SKI COUNTRY!

Nordic Skiers' Guide
to the
Minnesota Arrowhead

Robert Beymer

Library of Congress Card Catalog Number: 86-81167

International Standard Book Number: 0-933287-01-1

First edition

Printed in the United States of America

Published by W.A. Fisher Company

       123 Chestnut Street — Box 1107

       Virginia, Minnesota 55792-1107

PREFACE

During a December visit to Colorado, back in 1973, I was introduced to cross country skiing, sometimes called ski touring, sometimes called Nordic skiing. At that time, "skinny skis" were virtually unknown to most Americans. But the sport made a good first impression on me. For three good reasons: 1) Compared to Alpine (downhill) skiing, Nordic skiing is very inexpensive, both in terms of original outfitting and during continued performance; 2) There are no long lift lines and no crowded slopes for cross country skiers; and 3) Unlike Alpine skiers who are, more or less, confined to hillsides underneath ski lifts, cross country skiers have virtually unlimited freedom to explore the countryside — anywhere they wish.

After my introduction, I bought a pair of Asnes wooden skis, cane poles, metal bindings and leather boots — all for under $100. That gear is still in service and I consider the purchase one of the best bargains I have ever made. When I returned to my home in the Missouri Ozarks, I was one of the few people at that time to enjoy skiing in the Ozark highlands during the infrequent periods of heavy snowfall. I skied in southern Illinois and Iowa, too. But it wasn't until I moved to Minnesota that I truly became "hooked" on the sport.

In Minnesota (and probably all northern states, I suppose) people are generally divided into two groups: those who look forward to winter with eagerness, and those unfortunate souls who dread the white season and shed tears at the first sight of snow (often in September). Cross country skiers, of course, fall into the first category. Skiers are seldom afflicted with a mid-winter disease that strikes other folks — cabin fever. The sport of cross country skiing provides an excellent opportunity to 1) exercise during the "off season," 2) enjoy Mother Nature's winter splendor, and 3) breathe the freshest air of the entire year. If you're new to the sport, you are in for a real treat!

This book is little more than a gathering of information that is available to the public — literature from the U.S. Forest Service, the Minnesota Department of Natural Resources, various Chambers of Commerce, resort associations, ski clubs and individual ski lodges. To supplement that information, I talked with as many cross country skiing "authorities" as possible — forest service officials, resort owners, resident pros at ski lodges and avid skiers. Finally, I attempted to ski as many of the trails as my schedule (and the snow conditions) would allow. In some cases, when the snow was poor, I hiked trails to get a "feel" for what they have to offer skiers.

Prior to publication of this guide, there was no ONE comprehensive source of cross country ski information available to the public. As a former Twin Cities resident who sought new trails to explore each winter, I found the lack of a central source of information frustrating. Naturally, each resort association or chamber of commerce promoted its own local area, and that area was, of course, described as the best.

What I have done, therefore, is sandwich all of the trail descriptions and resort information between the covers of one book. In my opinion, the Arrowhead, as a whole, is the best ski country in America. And one of the nicest things about it is the diversity of trails that it has to offer skiers of all abilities.

Future additions of this book will be updated to include the latest improvements in existing trails, development of new trails, openings of new winter resort facilities, and any corrections to the current text. Although I have attempted to be as comprehensive as possible, it's entirely possible (indeed, PROBABLE) that I have missed a trail or inadvertently omitted a resort or other business that caters to cross country skiers in the Arrowhead. If so, I apologize in advance. Any suggestions for additions to, or corrections of, this text will be welcomed. Please write the author in care of the publisher. Thank you!

Robert Beymer
Ely, Minnesota
February, 1986

To the hardy people of arctic Norway

Who knew a great sport . . .

. . . Long before it was one.

ACKNOWLEDGMENTS

To be honest, I must confess that this project required considerably more research than I had thought it would. The deeper I dug into the subject, the more I discovered, which necessitated further digging. The hole grew deeper and deeper, until I was nearly buried in an avalanche of facts about the ski areas and lodging facilities of northeastern Minnesota. Every chamber of commerce, resort association, state park and Forest Service district office was contacted with a request for information. They, in turn, referred me to all of the ski clubs, resort owners and other people "in the know" about cross-country skiing in the Arrowhead region. Many, many people were eager to supply me with a wealth of skiing information. For that cooperation, I am grateful. Thanks to all of the people associated with the United States Forest Service in Superior National Forest, the state parks in the Arrowhead, all of the chambers of commerce and resort associations, and the individual resorts, motels and ski clubs who contributed to this guide. It's impossible to list all of the names . . .

A few people made special contributions to my project. To them, I offer my special thanks:

Steve Asche — Lutsen Ski Touring Center

Sandy Bodkin — Crane Lake Commerical Club

Harry Drabik & R.J. Novitsky — Grand Portage

Sharlene & Chuck Gecas — Heston's Country Store & Cabins

Brian Karich — Hibbing Joint Recreation & Park Board

Bruce & Susan Kerfoot — Gunflint Lodge

John Kuyava — La Croix District Ranger, USFS

George U. Nelson III — Lutsen Resort

Brian Olson — Grand Portage Lodge

Carla Peterson — The Village at Lutsen Mountains

Mike Rice — Bear Island Resort

Barb Soderberg — United States Forest Service, Duluth

My patient skiing models (in addition to those already mentioned): Shannon Bowers, Karen Corbin, Jacque Eggen, Ann & Kevin Hubbard, Mike Manlove, Mike Nagovan, Ray Niedzielski, Tim Rimer, Linda & Rolf Swanson, Check & Adel Tiffany, Joni Wartchow, Lynne Painter Wolf and Gayle Zullick.

Two other people deserve special recognition: Earl Fisher, for having enough faith in this project to publish the results; and Cheryl Beymer, whose 100% support both at home and on the trail has made this book a pleasure to produce.

CONTENTS

CHAPTER ONE

INTRODUCTION

Why ski the Arrowhead?

White frosted evergreens against the deep blue backdrop of a cloudless sky. Lovely white-tailed deer bounding through belly-deep white powder. Stately pines that were already one hundred feet tall when Thomas Jefferson authored the Declaration of Independence. Silence. Not even a whisper of wind through the pine needles, allowing snow to pile high in slendor columns upon the branches. An enormous moon that floods the landscape with sufficient light — soft, romantic light — to ski well into the night. The stillness interrupted momentarily by the mournful, solitary howling of a distant timber wolf. These are the sights and sounds and silences of a Northwoods winter.

Nowhere in North America is there a region more ideally suited to cross country skiing. Covered by the largest national forest in the lower forty-eight, this three-county area is characterized by a gently rolling landscape, cold, crisp days and an abundance of deep snow that persists from mid-December through at least the end of March. In a state that is full of excellent ski areas, perhaps born of the Nordic tradition that has influenced many aspects of Minnesota lifestyle, nowhere is the skiing better than in the Arrowhead. To many, in fact, winter is the most beautiful time of year in this lovely area that has long been attracting visitors during the other three seasons.'

But, shhhh! Don't tell anyone! This is a local secret. Winter is a time when the folks of northern Minnesota relax and recuperate from the hectic summer months — time to jealously enjoy the tranquility and incredible beauty of the Northwoods.

When word gets out about what this region has to offer cross country skiers, northeastern Minnesota will, some day, be a veritable Mecca for Nordic enthusiasts. It will, some day, be for Nordic skiers what central Colorado has already become for Alpine skiers. Ely, Grand Marais, Lutsen and Crane Lake will, some day, be as well known to winter recreationalists as are Aspen, Vail, Breckinridge and Steamboat Springs. Until that time comes, however, the secret is ours. We can enjoy the 800 miles of ski trails all to ourselves. No crowds. Bountiful wildlife. Quiet villages. And some of the most incredible scenery that Mother Nature has ever created.

Why ski the Arrowhead? Indeed, why not!

Winter Wonderland?

What is the Arrowhead

The Arrowhead is the name Minnesotans have given to the northeastern corner of Minnesota — a triangular wedge of real estate that borders Lake Superior on the southeast and the Canadian border on the north. The western border is not as clearly defined. The perimeter of the region included in this guide is more restrictive than that of the Arrowhead described by the Minnesota Office of Tourism. This guide includes only those ski trails that fall in the three northeasternmost counties of the state: Cook, Lake and St. Louis counties, excluding the Duluth metropolitan area. Included in this region are the North Shore of Lake Superior, all of Superior National Forest, including the Boundary Waters Canoe Area Wilderness, Voyageurs National Park, the state parks east of and including McCarthy Beach State Park, numerous state forests, and a large mining region known as the Iron Range. Except near the center of the Iron Range (known locally as The Range), it is a sparsely populated territory, where extensive land tracts are owned by the federal government, the state and the counties. This availability of public land for recreational purposes is one of the factors that makes the Arrowhead one of the best places in the United States for cross-country skiing.

Because of a preponderance of evergreens in the densely wooded forests of northeastern Minnesota, this boreal landscape is as lovely in winter as at any other time of the year. Dark green stands of spruce, pine and fir blend with a mixture of aspen, birch and maple trees to envelope skiers in a wonderland of Northwoods winter wildlife. The distinctive tracks of moose and white-tailed deer are common along most of the ski trails. Evidence of wolves is also seen, on occasion. Northeastern Minnesota harbors the only substantial population of timber wolves remaining in the contiguous forty-eight states. They feed primarily on deer and moose in winter, and skiers occasionally encounter "kill sites" along the ski trails. Snowshoe hares, ideally suited for Minnesota winters with natural snowshoes and white coats, are also common in some areas. The northern forests are far from dead in winter.

But the silence of winter is remarkable. On a calm day, after skiing deep into the woods, stop for a moment and listen. The only sound you may hear is the beating of your heart and the air forced out of your lungs. At times, the silence will be broken by the high-pitched chatter of a red squirrel or the flutter of a Canada Jay. But only for a moment. This degree of tranquillity is never attainable in the city . . .

Nowhere in North America is there a region more ideally suited to cross country skiing.

12

THE MINNESOTA ARROWHEAD

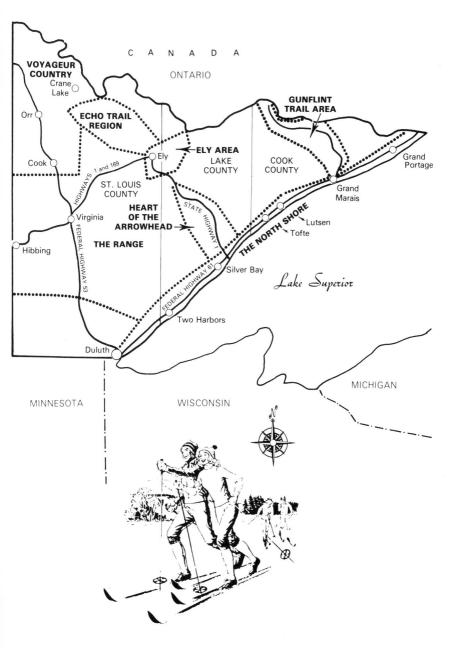

CANADA

VOYAGEUR
COUNTRY
Crane
Lake

ONTARIO

GUNFLINT
TRAIL AREA

Orr

ECHO TRAIL
REGION

ELY AREA
LAKE
COUNTY

COOK
COUNTY

Grand
Portage

Cook

Ely

HIGHWAYS 1 and 169

ST. LOUIS
COUNTY

Grand
Marais

STATE HIGHWAY 1

HEART
OF THE
ARROWHEAD

Virginia

Lutsen

THE NORTH SHORE

Tofte

THE RANGE

FEDERAL HIGHWAY 53

Hibbing

FEDERAL HIGHWAY 61

Silver Bay

Lake Superior

Two Harbors

Duluth

MINNESOTA

WISCONSIN

MICHIGAN

Climate: American Siberia or Winter Wonderland?

The climate of northeastern Minnesota is largely misunderstood by most southerners (that's anyone living south of Duluth). TV reports of the "coldest spot in the nation" frequently draw attention to such foreboding locations as International Falls, Hibbing and Embarrass. Those unfamiliar with the Northwoods winters envision a barren, arctic tundra, where roads are drifted closed most of the time, where general stores are stocked full in the fall to carry over through the long winter months, and where no sane person would venture outside unless an emergency warranted it absolutely necessary. This image is FAR from correct. Oh sure, Minnesota is a cold state in January and the first half of February. To someone who spent all of his or her life in Florida or Hawaii, the winter weather might just be unbearable. Granted. But, to people who live north of the Mason-Dixon line (that's probably YOU, since a real southerner wouldn't even pick up this book!), winter in northern Minnesota is not too harsh to tolerate. Except for a very few downright miserable days each year, when the temperature drops to -40^0 and the wind-chill dips to around -90^0F., the cool climate is ideally suited to cross country skiing. From mid-December through the end of March, the temperatures are just about right to maintain a good snow base for trails and a comfortable atmosphere for skiers.

Experienced skiers understand that skiing, like jogging, generates considerable body heat. With that in mind, it is not so crazy to suggest that ideal temperatures for cross country skiers range from 0^0F. to around 20^0F. Not only is it most comfortable in that range. It is also easiest to wax effectively.

Average daily high temperatures for the Arrowhead range from about 20^0 to 24^0 in December, 13^0 to 18^0 in January, and 23^0 to 27^0 in February (less than 20^0 during the first half of the month). The coldest temperatures are usually in the northwestern part of the region, while temperatures are somewhat warmer near Lake Superior, where the lake exerts a moderating effect on the climate. As a rule, the temperatures in Duluth are seldom more than 4 to 5 degrees colder than temperatures in the Twin Cities.

Low temperatures do occasionally hit extremes. In Ely, the coldest day of the year averages about -37^0F. normally, though not always, in January. Average lows, however, are considerably more moderate: around 8^0F. in December, 0 to -10^0F in January, and -2^0F to 3^0 in February.

For skiers who prefer the balmy spring weather, skiing is usually possible through the end of March and sometimes well into April. In March, high temperatures range from 32 to 36^0F., while lows range from 10 to 16^0F.

Snow depths are generally the greatest a short distance inland from the shore of Lake Superior and near the Laurentian Highlands (the north-south continental divide). Average snowfall for Duluth is 78 inches, while Ely averages about 63 inches. In the higher region along the Laurentian Highlands (like up the Gunflint Trail), 100 inches of snow is not unusual. By mountain standards, this is not an extraordinary amount. But excessive snow is detrimental to cross country skiers who prefer to break their own

American Siberia?

trails. In the Northwoods, a good skiing base is maintained throughout the long winters. And mid-winter thaws are seldom long enough to seriously damage the snow base for skiers.

Access to ski trails is also no problem. In the Arrowhead, contrary to public perception, state and county roads are usually much better than in the Twin Cities metropolitan area following snow storms. The only roads that are not plowed regularly are Forest Roads along which there are no permanent winter residents. These unplowed roads, in fact, provide excellent skiing routes in much of Superior National Forest. With a few easy precautions for you and your automobile, there is no reason why winter in northeastern Minnesota should be a hardship — even to a southerner. (See tips on page 24.)

American Siberia? No, this magnificent region is definitely a winter wonderland!

Arrowhead roads are nearly always in good winter driving condition.

CHAPTER TWO

HOW TO USE THIS GUIDE

This book is a compilation of all the designated cross-country ski trails in the Arrowhead region of northeastern Minnesota. The key word here is "designated." Like walking, ski touring can take place virtually anywhere, from city parks to deep within the Boundary Waters Canoe Area Wilderness. In fact, the BWCAW is, itself, a source of unlimited ski trips across hundreds of lakes and portage trails that have been used·as water routes during the ice-free season for hundreds of years. Likewise, any logging road or Forest Route in Superior National Forest that is not plowed in winter is a potential ski trail. There are hundreds of miles of such roads in Cook, St. Louis and Lake counties. To reference them all would take another volume. All one needs to "designate" one's own cross-country ski trails are a Superior Forest map, a good imagination and a healthy dose of common sense.

The trails included in this guide, on the other hand, are those that have been specifically designated by the Forest Service, resort owners and ski associations for use by cross country skiers. Most of them were designed specifically for skiers, and many of them are machine groomed and track-set to permit optimum skiing conditions in the deep snow of the Arrowhead. In contrast, some trails were not constructed with skiers in mind, are used mostly by summertime hikers and are not machine groomed and tracked. Nevertheless, they are considered to be good ski routes for those who don't need the "security" of established tracks.

Regardless of the type of trail, this guide treats them all the same. First, the trails are grouped by geographic location. The entire Arrowhead is divided into seven regions: the North Shore, the Gunflint Trail, the Heart of the Arrowhead, the Ely Area, the Echo Trail Region, Voyageur Country and The Range. Following a brief general description of a region, the ski trails contained within that region are described individually. The description begins with a quick overview that includes: 1) use level, 2) type of trail, 3) difficulty, 4) length, 5) maps needed and where to get them, 6) highlights of the trail, and 7) the trailhead location. Following that introduction is a brief description, informing the reader about the general character of the trail. Finally, the trail system, itself, is analyzed in sufficient detail to give the reader a good idea of what to expect along the way. After reading an entire trail profile, a skier should have a good idea if the trail is suitable for him or her.

Since relatively few skiers are also winter campers, the book goes on to list and describe the lodging accommodations available in the vicinity of each trail. Discussion includes a quick overview of the facilities that are offered, followed by a general description of the resort and the special attractions that it offers its guests. Addresses and phone numbers are included, so that potential guests may contact the resorts directly for additional information.

Machine grooming with a track-setter creates superb ski trails throughout the winter season.

Windfalls are not uncommon on "natural environment" trails.

Selecting a Ski Trail

Perhaps the best thing about skiing in the Arrowhead Region is the diversity of trails for all types of skiers. Most development has occurred in Cook County in the tip of the Arrowhead. That small county accounts for nearly half of the trail mileage included in this guide, and over 60% of the machine groomed and tracked trails in the Arrowhead. No other county in this state — or any other state, for that matter — has such a superb network of nicely groomed trails amidst scenery as beautiful as that found there. Along the North Shore of Lake Superior are two outstanding trail networks: the North Shore Mountains Trail, and the Grand Portage Reservation trails. Up the Gunflint Trail is another splendid network of interconnected trails extending from East Bearskin Lake northwest to the Canadian border at Gunflint Lake. These three systems alone include over 300 miles of groomed trails passing over a good variety of terrain that will satisfy any cross country skier — first-timer to expert.

Along with a well-developed system of groomed trails is also a well developed congregation of four-season resorts that offers a pleasing choice of accommodations for skiers. Unique to this area is the lodge-to-lodge "ski-through" program that permits skiers to ski from one resort to another to experience a variety of lodging accommodations. The participating resorts shuttle the skiers' luggage from one lodge to the next and provide trail lunches for the skiers. This is the best way for skiers to experience the widest possible assortment of both the ski trails and the lodging accommodations. All of the North Shore Mountains and the Gunflint Trail system may now be enjoyed in this way.

The trails in Lake and St. Louis counties are not as concentrated as those in Cook County. Nor are they as well developed. Currently, there are no "ski-through" programs available. Nevertheless, it would be a BIG mistake to overlook them. Unlike the trail coordination in Cook County there has been little, if any, attempt in the past to develop any large trail systems that would rival those in the tip of the Arrowhead. But progress is currently being made. In the southern part of Lake County, the Suomi Ski Club is planning to coordinate a network of trails that may someday join the North Shore Mountains system with Crosby Manitou State Park, the Finland area trails, Tettegouche State Park and the Northwoods Ski Trail. At the north end of the county, a similar plan is underway to join the separate trail systems at Jasper Hills, Flash Lake, Lake One and the Fernberg Tower into a large network of groomed trails. The Ashawa Ski Trail, when completed, will make a 39-mile loop around the west end of Lake Vermilion, near Cook in St. Louis County.

St. Louis County offers a tremendous variety of cross country ski trails. In the northern part of the county, on either side of the Echo Trail (County Road 116), most of the ski trails are classified as "natural environment" trails. They are not machine groomed and track-set, and they penetrate the seldom-visited, pristine interior of the Boundary Waters Canoe Area Wilderness. In the Range district of central St. Louis County, on the other hand, there are a number of superbly groomed trail systems that receive frequent visitors from nearby population centers. Most notable is the new Giants Ridge Ski Area, near Biwabik, where excellent trails lead to panoramic vistas from atop the Laurentian Divide.

Which areas are best? For some skiers, the "best" trails are the ones that have expertly manicured sets of tracks. For others, "best" implies long, fast hills. Yet "best" could also mean no hills at all. It might also mean no tracks at all — and no chance of seeing other people during the skiing experience. In northeastern Minnesota, the options are many, and that's what makes the Arrowhead the BEST.

To help you identify the trail options available to you, APPENDIX I alphabetically lists all of the 61 designated ski areas in the Arrowhead. It also identifies the geographic region in which each trail is located, its length, its difficulty, and whether or not it is machine groomed and track-set. Finally, it references the page number on which there is a detailed discussion of the trail. Use APPENDIX I to focus on the types of trails that are considered appropriate for your skills and time schedule.

Which trail is best for you? Only you can decide . . .

A Kassbohrer Pisten Bully groomer is used at Grand Portage to "manufacture" trails that are second to none.

State Ski Licenses are available at the headquarters of Arrowhead state parks.

North Country Lodging

For many skiers, an important part of their weekend outing or winter vacation — perhaps even more important than the trails — is their lodging accommodations. Considering that fact, this guide includes descriptions of all the lodging facilities in the Arrowhead region that have expressed a desire to cater to cross country skiers. Many of them are directly linked to one or more of the ski trails. At some, a skier may ski directly from one's cabin to the trails. At others, shuttle service is provided from the room to the trailhead.

When a resort is directly linked to a particular trail or system of trails, the description of that resort immediately follows the description of the corresponding trail. For instance, the discussion of "Grand Portage Lodge" is directly preceded by the discussion of the "Grand Portage Area Trails." On the other hand, when lodging is not directly related to a particular trail, it is listed with similar resorts and motels at the conclusion of the chapter dealing with the geographic region in which the lodging is located. For instance, "Ely Area Lodging" concludes the chapter on "Ely Area Ski Trails." And so forth . . .

APPENDIX II summarizes the lodging facilities that cater to Arrowhead skiers. It lists each resort and motel alphabetically, identifies the geographic region in which it is located, summarizes the type of lodging units and amenities that are available and, finally, references the page number on which more information can be found. Use APPENDIX II as a quick reference to the lodging options that are appropriate to your needs.

Heavy Use Periods

Arrowhead skiing is largely a weekend phenomenon. None of the ski trails is crowded on weekdays. In fact, very few trails receive any more than the lightest use then. But some weekends can be quite different. Christmas to New Year's Day, and the Presidents' Day Weekend are the busiest holidays for ski resorts. If you plan a trip to the Arrowhead for either of those periods, make plans far in advance — perhaps even a year ahead at some resorts.

But, even during the busiest holiday weekends, skiers are not likely to feel crowded on any of the Arrowhead trails. Someday, this region will be discovered by America. Americans will learn what a splendid region this is for winter recreation. Meanwhile, it's a secret that you can take advantage of: peaceful trails winding through lovely Northwoods wilderness; few people; good opportunities for seeing wildlife.

The ski areas that receive the most people are generally the systems that are large enough to adequately disburse those people in all directions. The result is a peaceful skiing experience for all.

Standards for Trail Ratings

The description of each ski trail begins with three summarizations: Use Level, Trail Type and Difficulty. All three are based on subjective analyses, partly from personal observations and partly from the recommendations of the Forest Service, Park Ranger, or organization responsible for developing and/or maintaining the trails. Since the ratings are subjective, you need to know how they are determined.

USE LEVEL: None of the trails in the Arrowhead region is crowded — at any time — compared to some popular city trails in Duluth or Minneapolis, or to the Hennepin County trails that surround the Twin Cities, for instance. Seldom is it likely that you will bump elbows with other skiers or wait in line to herringbone up a steep hill — even on holiday weekends! In fact, nearly all of the trails in the Arrowhead region would have to be rated "light" on weekdays. The ratings mentioned in this book, however, are for the "average" weekend in January and February, when the trails receive most of their use. This is what you might expect with each of the ratings:

LIGHT: Seldom will you encounter any other people along the trails. Skiers are likely to feel a sense of true wilderness isolation while skiing.

MODERATE: Although crowds are certainly not a problem, it is likely that you will encounter other people occasionally. While sking downhill runs, be alert to the possibility of uphill traffic coming against you.

HEAVY: Very few trails ever receive heavy use in the Arrowhead. It means that you are likely to see other people most of the time. Downhill runs may be hazardous because of other people on the trails. Whenever a skier stops to rest, or falls, he or she must immediately get off the trail to allow other skiers to pass.

TRAIL TYPE: Most Arrowhead ski trails fall into one of two categories. Either they are machine groomed and track-set, or they are "natural environment" trails that are not groomed and tracked by machines. Depending on the degree of use, natural environment trails may either be across unbroken snow, or with tracks that have been made by previous skiers. If it has been skied frequently by good skiers, a natural environment trail may have tracks that are nearly as good as those created by machines.

But even machine groomed trails will vary considerably in quality. The ultimate track-setter is the Kassbohrer Pisten-Bully groomer, which enables superb trails even during poor snow conditions. This machine is used on three trail systems in the Arrowhead: the Central Gunflint Trails around Bearskin Lodge, the Giants Ridge Ski Area and the Grand Portage Area Trails.

Novice skiers will probably have an easier experience on nicely groomed trails. After the basic skills are mastered, however, one may quickly "graduate" to the natural environment trails.

In considering the type of trail that is suitable for your skill level, it is important to remember one very important point. There is a wide variety of trails included in this guide. Ski touring on groomed and tracked trails is as different from breaking a new trail through deep snow as jogging is from backpacking. The former can be done quickly and smoothly, with as little effort expended as one desires. The latter is a slow, deliberate, plodding method to escape from the beaten path. One does not glide smoothly and quickly through the woods in deep, unbroken snow, just as a backpacker is not likely to jog over the trails he follows. They are totally different kinds of experiences. Some skiers prefer "jogging." Others tend toward "backpacking." One is not better than the other, just different. Apples and oranges . . .

DIFFICULTY: This category may be the most important for you to select the trail that is suitable for your skills. Standards vary considerably from one trail system to the next. A trail that is rated "easiest" at one area might be rated "more difficult" at another area. This guide rates all of the trails in the Arrowhead region according to the following criteria:

BEGINNER: For the person who has just learned to ski and who feels uncomfortable skiing on any terrain more hilly than a Kansas wheat field. The only hills are very gently sloping, and there are no sharp turns thrown in for excitement.

ADVANCED BEGINNER: For the inexperienced skier who is finally getting bored with flat terrain and is ready to graduate to an Iowa landscape with rolling hills and gentle turns.

INTERMEDIATE: For the skier who has mastered all of the basic skiing skills, is looking for a little excitement on the course, and can handle short, steep hills or long gradual slopes.

ADVANCED: For the skier who likes good downhill runs and can handle steep uphill grades. Excitement is the word. Plenty of action for the experienced skier. The more mountainous the better.

22

CHAPTER 3

INTRODUCTION TO CROSS COUNTRY SKIING

"If you can walk, you can cross country ski!" That's a proclamation made by many ski instructors at the beginning of instruction. A bit over-simplified, perhaps. But the underlying premise is true: learning to cross country ski is easy. Kids can do it. Mom and dad can learn. And, yes, even grandmas and grandpas can learn to enjoy Nordic skiing. It is a sport for all ages, for all income levels, and for all degrees of athletic ability. To get started, one needs only to invest a small amount in equipment and to learn a few of the fundamentals. Proficiency will result from practice.

This chapter will introduce you to the basics — courtesy, safety, equipment, clothing, waxing and special regulations. Like any sport, skiing can most easily be learned from coaching by a person with experience. Practice in your own back yard or at a nearby municipal golf course. After you have learned the basics, you will be ready to head for Ski Country.

Trail Courtesy

Although trail use is normally light in the Arrowhead, the trails on which you ski will, at one time or another, be used by other skiers. Common courtesy for others should be automatic. Novice skiers, however, may not be familiar with some of the special rules of skiing etiquette. And, even for the "old pros," it never hurts to review them . . .

The United States Ski Association suggests the following six considerations:

1) RESPECT FOR OTHERS: A cross country skier must ski in such a manner that he does not endanger or prejudice others.

2) RESPECT FOR SIGNS: Trail marking signs must be respected on any trail marked with an indicated direction for travel; a skier shall proceed only in that direction.

3) OVERTAKING: The skier ahead is not obliged to give way to an overtaking skier, but should allow a faster skier to pass whenever he judges it possible. A skier is permitted to overtake and pass another skier to the left or right, either in a free track or outside the tracks.

4) ENCOUNTER: Cross-country skiers meeting while skiing in opposite directions shall keep to the right. A climbing skier shall give way to a descending skier.

5) POLES: A cross country skier shall keep his poles close to his body whenever near another skier.

6) CONTROL OF SPEED: A cross country skier, especially when skiing downhill, shall always adapt his speed to his personal ability, to the prevailing terrain and visibility, and to the traffic on the course. Every skier should keep a safe distance from the skiers ahead. As a last resort, an intentional fall should be used to avoid a collision.

In addition to the USSA suggestions, here are a few more points to consider:

7) MAINTAINING GOOD TRACKS: If you should fall, help maintain the tracks by filling in holes and resetting the tracks. And, if you must walk through a difficult portion of the trail, be sure to walk OFF to the side of the trail, to not ruin the tracks for others.

8) PETS: Dogs are great companions for outdoor activities. BUT, they don't belong on groomed trails! Unless you can train your dog to walk off to the side of the trail and to never step in front of a skier, leave the loveable beast at home. If you are too emotionally involved with your pet to leave it at home, then maintain control at all times, reset the ski tracks after it, and by all means, clean up any "brown klister" that may be left in the track.

9) PRIVATE PROPERTY: Don't ski on private property, unless it is crossed by a designated and approved ski trail. Avoid skiing near cabins or across any property where water pipes are likely to be buried. Compressing the snow above ground containing water pipes will drive the frost deeper, and may result in frozen pipes. Deep snow insulates the ground and prevents the pipes from freezing.

10) LITTER: Be sure to carry out all litter. Hiding it in the snow won't appeal to hikers next summer!

11) PERSONAL HYGENE: OK, it happens to even the most experienced skiers. Nothing to be ashamed of. But, if you must relieve yourself while out skiing, do so away from the trail. Those who follow will be grateful! No one wants to see yellow snow.

Tips for Safety and Comfort

Common sense and good preparation are ESSENTIAL to any winter outdoor activities. That applies double to ski touring in wilderness areas like the Arrowhead. Know your limitations. Study the weather forecasts. Familiarize yourself with the trails and local conditions BEFORE you set out. It is imperative that you be prepared for the unexpected. Winter is a gorgeous time of year for outdoor recreation. Indeed, it's a shame to NOT enjoy the snow-covered wilderness trails. But Mother Nature can be harsh to those who are ill-prepared to accept her on her own terms. An accident or an error in judgement that occurs in your own backyard may result in nothing more than a good lesson and maybe a little embarrassment. On a wilderness trail in northern Minnesota, however, the same accident or error could result in a life-threatening disaster.

Before heading into the back country in wintertime, consider the following tips for safety and personal comfort.

AUTOMOBILE PREPARATIONS: Before heading north, be certain that your car is ready for the trip. To be safe, cars should be winterized for at least −40° temperatures. Though the temperature is seldom that cold in the Arrowhead, it is likely to happen at least once during the winter. Supplying your car with adequate antifreeze, 5-W-30 motor oil and gas line antifreeze is cheap insurance. An engine block heater is also useful, and a good, strong battery is a must. Carry jumper cables and carburetor starting fluid (ether), too.

During the most severe winter weather, even the best of batteries may freeze overnight. During your stay in the Arrowhead, when extreme temperatures exist, it may be wise to remove the battery from your car and place it in your cabin or motel room, until you're ready to pack up and head for home.

SKI TRAVEL: As for any outdoor winter recreation, it is important to eat and sleep well BEFORE your ski outing. Never ski alone! And don't over-exert. Just moving around with warm clothing in cold weather is exhausting. Pay attention to the trail markers that indicate the level of trail difficulty. Don't take chances by attempting to exceed the limits of your ability. If you are not sure of your ability to safely negotiate a particular section of trail, remove your skis and walk along the edge of the trail until you reach a section that you know you can safely negotiate with skis. Prior to any outing, make certain that someone knows your route itinerary and has instructions to contact authorities if your return is overdue.

FINDING DIRECTIONS: The best way to avoid getting lost is to stay on marked trails unless you are experienced in wintertime cross country travel. At all times, carry a good map and a reliable compass — and know how to use them! Keep them both handy, and refer to them frequently, to keep track of your precise location. Compass needles, however, are sometimes fooled by massive iron ore deposits near the earth's surface in the Arrowhead. Common sense should always prevail. Knowing the general "lay of the land" will help considerably if you become lost. Knowledge of the general direction of stream flowage and the orientation of dominate ridges (usually a northeast to southwest pattern) could help as much as reading a compass.

Above all, at the first indication of being lost, stop. Try to refrain from panic. Analyze your predicament. If strong winds or newly fallen snow have not obscured your tracks, simply turn around and backtrack to your point of origin. If this is not possible, seek shelter, build a smokey warming fire and wait for someone to find you.

PERSONAL COMFORT: When penetrating the wilderness, always carry a small day pack ("fanny" pack is ideal) with a few basic survival articles and extra clothing: map and compass, knife, matches, candle, water bottle, high-energy snacks, spare ski tip(s), spare down jacket or vest, spare socks, toilet paper, and an emergency tube tent or "space blanket." A small, rectangular piece of styrofoam insulation serves as a good pack liner (between your back and the gear in the pack), and also provides a warm seat during rest stops. Use vaseline on the face and lips, and wear dark glasses to guard against the bright, reflecting sun.

Dress in layers of clothing, and be prepared for sudden changes of weather. Protect your head and neck: when they are warm, usually your whole body is warm. Guard against hypothermia and periodically observe your companion(s) for signs of frostbite.

Avoid excess tiring by not over estimating your abilities to travel long distances. Drink plenty of water and eat high-energy snacks at frequent intervals while skiing. Never drink alcohol! The apparent "warming" effects of alcohol are misleading, actually lowering your resistance to the cold.

DANGER SPOTS: Some of the trails in the Arrowhead were not originally designed for skiers, particularly in the Echo Trail Region. The ski routes may follow old portage paths, hiking trails or abandoned logging roads. Rocks, stumps and fallen trees may be hazards when there is insufficient snowfall to "cushion" the trails. Other ski routes utilize the frozen surfaces of lakes and streams. Be alert to streams and lakes that are not completely frozen. Layers of snow can insulate still water sufficiently to keep it from freezing solid. Springs, running water or decaying organic matter may also weaken the ice. On lakes, it is generally safest away from the shoreline and any jutting points. When lakes and rivers are covered with a thick layer of ice and snow, slush is a potential hazard. It's best to follow an existing trail, where the packed down snow is less likely to conceal slush.

SURVIVAL TIPS: Before heading into the wilderness, it is imperative that you are prepared to build a fire. Matches will do you little good if you don't know how to use them. Should you become lost, injured, exhausted, or drenched, the difference between life and death may depend on your ability to build a fire and to keep warm. If you have left your travel plans with someone back home or at the lodge, with instructions to contact authorities should you be overdue, there is little doubt that you will be found. Starvation is not a concern. Nor is dehydration, if the rescue occurs quickly. Freezing to death, however, *is* a concern. A warm fire could be a lifesaver, and the smoke from it will act as a signal to rescuers. Keep your matches in a waterproof container in a pocket or day pack. Use a wad of toilet paper to ignite the fire. Look for the dead, dry twigs and lower branches of spruce trees to use for kindling. Small dead trees that are leaning, but not touching the ground, provide the best firewood. Wood that is lying on the ground may look and snap like dry wood, but it is likely to have moisture frozen in it. Fire releases the moisture, and the wood is slow to ignite. Keep the fire small, away from shrubbery, not underneath snow-laden branches, and, if possible, against a rock mass. Like a stone fireplace, a rock mass will absorb heat and continue to radiate heat after the fire dies down. A small fire permits you to sit close enough to warm the whole body. A large bonfire will force you to move away. While one side of your body is hot, the dark side will be cold.

Snow piles high on branches — and nests — in tne wind-sheltered forests of the Northwoods.

First Aid for Skiers

Any accident that can happen to a person in summertime can also occur in winter. This book is not intended as a first aid primer. It's a good idea, however, for all back country trail users, whether in summer or in winter, to know the basics of first aid. The dangers are accentuated in winter. A broken ankle in summer time is not likely to be life-threatening. It's simply a matter of waiting as comfortably as possible until transportation arrives. In winter, however, the act of waiting can, itself, be life-threatening, if the temperature is well below zero and the victim is not prepared for waiting.

There are two afflictions that winter outdoor recreationalists must always be alert to: hypothermia and frostbite. Neither is likely to occur suddenly and dramatically, such as the breaking of a bone. They may stalk and gradually overwhelm them.

HYPOTHERMIA

Hypothermia is a dangerous loss of body heat caused by exposure to the cold. The onset is hastened by physical exhaustion, windy weather and the wearing of damp clothing. It is NOT the same as freezing though the end result may be the same — death. Hypothermia may occur at temperatures well above freezing, when conditions are just "right" to cause the body to lose heat faster than it is generated. We've all experienced mild cases — shivering and purple lips after swimming too long in cold water. If normal body temperature cannot be restored, however, the shivering may become violent, coordination may be lost, and death could result.

More often than not, hypothermia victims are wearing wet clothing. Wet clothing doesn't insulate nearly as well as dry clothing. Wool does the best when wet. Garments made of goose down, which is an excellent insulator when dry, lose nearly all of their insulating qualities when wet. At the first indication of hypothermia, therefore, it is important to exchange the wet clothing for dry clothing. Better yet, avoid wet clothing by layering your clothes (See Dressing For Ski Touring).

If hypothermia has alread struck, quickly get the victim into dry clothing. If that's not possible, place the victim near a fire and provide him with high-energy foods and warm drinks. If a warm sleeping bag is available, the best treatment is to put the victim into it along with another person, both naked so that body heat can be shared.

FROSTBITE

Frostbite, on the other hand, IS freezing. It results when inadquately protected flesh is exposed to the cold and wind for too long a period. The result is damaged or destroyed flesh tissue. Extreme cases may result in the loss of toes or fingers. Even mild cases may result in increased sensitivity to the cold and some painful memories. How long is too long? That depends on how cold it is and how hard the wind is blowing. At 30°F., with a 25 mph wind, the equivalent "wind-chill" temperature is 0°F. That can be dangerous, though not extreme. At 10°F., a 25 mph wind speed produces a −30°F. wind-chill temperature. Under that condition, exposed flesh may freeze in 1 minute. At 30° below zero, a 25 mph wind speed is equivalent to a −90°F. wind-chill temperature. In such conditions, exposed flesh may freeze in less than 30 seconds. Obviously, if you are skiing in such harsh weather conditions, you must have **no** exposed skin.

How do you know if you or someone else in your group is suffering from frostbite? As frostbite develops, the skin becomes grayish, white or yellowish-gray in appearance. The frostbitten skin will feel very cold or numb, and pain may or may not be present. Often, a victim is not even aware that he or she is afflicted with frostbite. That's why it is important to observe members of your group periodically, especially under extreme weather conditions and when there is a strong wind. As the affliction progresses, blisters may appear on the skin, and mental confusion may result. Ultimately, the body may suffer from extreme shock and death will occur.

Obviously, first aid involves getting the victim out of the cold and to warm the affected area. If conscious, the victim can be given warm fluids. If possible, put the affected area in warm water, but **not** hot water. Rubbing the area may do harm to the skin, even causing gangrene. After the affected area is warmed, have the victim exercise that part of the body.

Technique

In the introduction to this chapter, it was asserted that cross country skiing is easy; "If you can walk, you can cross country ski" — remember? It's true. But telling someone how in just a few words is not easy. In fact, telling someone how is not easy in any number of words. You can read about tennis, or handball or cross country skiing until you're sick of facts and illustrations about techniques. But, until you actually get into gear and try the sport, learning is impossible. The best way to learn the proper techniques of cross country skiing is to employ the services of a qualified instructor. One full hour of competent instruction should be sufficient to learn enough of the fundamentals to hit the trails and really enjoy the sport. Proficiency will result from practice. Special techniques can be learned when special situations arise. Until the time arrives when you have mastered all of the techniques, you can literally side-step an uncomfortable situation (steep climb or steep descent, etc.) by removing your skis and walking around the obstacle. The most important thing to remember is this: know your limitations! And ski in a manner that is appropriate to those limitations.

Many books have been written to impart the "how to" of cross country skiing. This is not one of them. Consult your ski shop, camping outfitter or local library. Three books that you might consider for an introduction to the sport are:

Bennett, Margaret: CROSS COUNTRY SKIING FOR THE FUN OF IT. New York: Dodd, Mead and Company, 1973.

Brady, Michael: NORDIC TOURING AND CROSS COUNTRY SKIING. Oslo: Dreyer, 1979 (Fifth revised edition). Distributed by Wilderness Press, 2440 Bancroft Way, Berkeley, CA 94704.

Heller, Mark and Godlington, Doug — Editors: THE COMPLETE SKIING HANDBOOK. New York: Mayflower Books, Inc., 1979.

Get Into Gear

One needs to invest only a small amount in equipment to get started in the sport of cross country skiing. All the gear you need may be rented at ski resorts or from shops in towns all over the Arrowhead. Weekend rates are usually quite reasonable. But, then, so is the cost of new equipment. After you have tried cross country skiing once, you will surely be hooked on the sport. At that point, it is advisable to buy your own gear (new or used), because rental fees will quickly add up to the purchase price of a new set of equipment.

When you are ready to buy, consult a reputable dealer, ask friends for recommendations, and consider your own propensity for maintenance. Here are just a few tips to consider when selecting gear to use in the Arrowhead.

SKIS: Your first choice is whether to use waxable skis or no-wax skis (See WAXING on page 31). If you are the type of person who strives for the highest possible performance, and you don't mind spending time and energy to achieve that performance, go with waxable skis. On the other hand, if you prefer to not mess around with maintenance and the preparation of your ski bases, and high performance is not a goal, you may find no-wax skis more practical.

If skiing will be done almost exclusively on machine groomed and track-set trails, "light touring" skis are the most appropriate. If, on the other hand, you plan to ski primarily on "natural environment trails" that are not groomed and probably not tracked, wider "touring" skis are preferable. Beginners will find greater stability on the wider touring skis.

The length of your skis should be about 12" to 14" more than your height. A ski that is not too rigid and has only a moderate amount of camber is easier for a novice to control. Gliding speed will be somewhat slower, but the skier's ability to grip the snow on hills will be enhanced. Most beginners are not reluctant to sacrifice speed for control!

BOOTS: Over-the-ankle ski boots offer the most support and stability for beginners and for those who ski off the designated trails through unbroken snow. They also tend to be warmer than low-cut shoes. Boots with plastic molded soles and leather uppers that breathe are preferable to all-synthetic shoes. When being fitted, be sure to wear the same two pairs of socks that you will be wearing while skiing, and allow plenty of room for toe movement.

BINDINGS: The traditional larger bindings with sides to protect your shoes are most practical for skiing through rough wilderness terrain. For control on downhill turns, be certain that there are good grip plates under the heels of your boots. These will help hold your feet in the proper placement on the skis.

POLES: Poles may be made from either bamboo or fiberglass, with cork or roughened leather grips. Be certain that the wrist loops afford adquate room for comfort when you are wearing mittens or gloves. When standing vertically on the ground, the poles should reach to your armpits.

An experienced skier is prepared to wax for any and all snow conditions.

Waxing

Unlike Alpine skis, cross country skis must be able to grip, as well as to glide. It is that dual capacity to grip and glide that enables skiers to travel easily across level terrain and to even climb hills. Some use wax to accomplish both objectives, while others rely on surface irregularities in the ski bases that permit both gliding and gripping.

The debate over whether to use waxable skis or no-wax skis goes far beyond the practical aspects that either can offer. To many skiers, it is tangible evidence of one's recreational philosophy. It is a question not unlike whether to use wooden skis or synthetics, silk underwear or polypropylene, woolens or synthetic pile garments — "natural" versus man-made substitutes. Only you can decide what is most suitable for your spiritual well-being.

If you are a novice, however, you might consider the practical aspects of waxable and no-wax skis. Like so many things in this complex world, what is best for one person may not be right for another. For the high-performance skier, there is really no substitute for proper waxing. For the beginner, however, or for the person who has little interest in "prep time," no-wax skis may be the most appropriate choice. Skiers using no-wax skis are ready to ski at a moment's notice, regardless of the snow conditions (more on "conditions" later). Performance will be relatively consistent, and there is no chance of frustration from improper waxing. No-wax skis are appreciated the most on days when snow conditions change frequently. Trails that are exposed to bright sunlight in some places, while heavily shaded in other spots, are particularly difficult to wax for. Likewise, on days when the temperature fluctuates from below freezing to above freezing temperatures, effective waxing is a chore. The no-wax skier, on the other hand, is not adversely affected.

Nevertheless, when temperatures are consistently well below freezing, as is customary in the Arrowhead during the months of January and February, waxing is not as difficult as many people are led to believe. Although there are dozens of different waxes available to high-performance skiers, the average recreational skier seldom needs more than three or four different waxes during mid-winter.

The proper wax to use for cross country skiing depends on three variables: 1) the type of snow (fresh snow versus old settled snow, for instance), 2) the temperature (softer waxes for warmer temperatures), and 3) the moisture of the snow (at 32°F., it may be either dry or quite wet). Waxes are color coded to indicate the temperature range for which they are recommended. Instructions are also written on the side of the wax container to indicate the types of snow for which they are intended.

When a ski stops under the weight of a skier, the snow crystals penetrate the wax to grip the base of the ski. Then,, when the ski is moved forward, the crystals are wiped off the base and the skier is able to glide smoothly and quickly. If the wax is too soft for the type of snow, the crystals will penetrate too deeply and not release for a smooth glide. On the other hand, if the wax is too hard, the snow crystals may not penetrate the wax at all, and the ski will slip backwards when the skier pushes off.

Under normal circumstances, when preparing to ski in the Arrowhead in mid-winter, plan on cold, dry snow. The three waxes most commonly used then are polar (white), green and blue. These three waxes will take care of most temperatures and snow conditions from the mid-20's on down. If crusty, icy conditions prevail, however, a blue klister may also be needed (such as following a mid-winter thaw).

Spring skiing requires additional waxes. Blue (even green) wax may be appropriate in early morning hours. But, as the temperature quickly rises above the freezing point, softer waxes are necessary. Red, violet, yellow and red klister waxes are often used in the spring (March and early April).

Learning to wax effectively takes practice. But it isn't all that difficult. There is a great little booklet on the market that is small enough to carry in your pocket. It is full of valuable information for the inexperienced skier who wants to master the techniques of waxing:

Brady & Skjemstad: WAXING FOR CROSS-COUNTRY SKIING. Wilderness Press(2440 Bancroft Way, Berkeley, CA 94704). A 2-page wax table shows the right kind of wax in every major brand to use for each possible set of snow conditions.

A torch is a useful tool for applying klister wax, for spring skiing in the Arrowhead.

Dressing For Ski Touring

The varying degrees of energy required for cross-country skiing, combined with the wide variety of winter temperatures possible in the Minnesota Arrowhead, makes LAYERING imperative. Layering permits skiers to stay warm enough, without over-heating. A novice may concern himself too much with the desire to stay warm in the frigid Minnesota climate. Experienced skiers, however, know that the biggest problem while cross-country skiing is avoiding OVER-heating. Brisk skiing, even in sub-zero temperatures, requires VERY little insulation from the cold. Allowing oneself to overheat often results in excessive perspiration that will absorb into one's clothing and eventually cause chilling. Ironically, over-heating usually results in chilling; and that can result in hypothermia, which can be deadly.

The **concept** of layering is the same for everyone and every situation. What the layers are, however, will vary from person to person and depend on a number of factors, including temperature and wind velocity. Essentially, there are three different kinds of layers required to keep warm and comfortable: 1) an inner layer that "breathes" and "wicks" moisture away from the body, 2) a middle layer (or layers) that traps still air, and 3) an outer layer that keeps out wind and moisture.

LAYER 1:   "Wicking" is the ability of some fibers to draw moisture away from the skin and pass it on to the next layer of clothing. Wool and silk have long been used for this purpose. But probably the best is polypropylene — plastic fibers that absorb no moisture. One of the worst is cotton. It absorbs and holds moisture. A damp layer of clothing next to the skin causes rapid chilling during rest stops. Polypropylene is used to make long underwear, socks, stocking caps and even glove liners. Next to you, "wicking" is the most important element of skiing comfort.

LAYER 2:   When air is trapped into small "pockets", it is easily warmed by the body. Some of the best insulators are wool, synthetic fleece, pile fabrics and goose down. The second layer includes a shirt or sweater, pants or knickers, socks, gloves and a hat. Additional inner layers will depend on the temperature, one's own unique ability to keep warm and how much energy is being exerted (uphill, downhill or on the level, for instance). A down vest over a wool sweater is ideal for skiing in extremely cold weather. Even if the vest is not needed while skiing, it is useful during rest stops.

LAYER 3:   An ideal outer fabric is one that "breathes," to let perspiration escape into the air, yet is water resistant enough to keep out moisture from wet snow. Hooded mountain parkas, anoraks or wind shells made from Gore-Tex, Storm Shed, or Ramar serve well in this capacity. In addition to the parka, this outer layer might include pants for harsh weather conditions. Gaiters help keep the feet and ankles warm by preventing snow from entering shoes. When weather is harsh, a face mask may also be necessary to prevent frostbite.

By pealing off or adding on layers of clothing, a skier will maintain a comfortable body temperature, regardless of the amount of energy exerted. In case of injury or excessive fatigue, always carry enough clothing for adequate protection during prolonged periods of rest.

Skiers who purchase State Ski Licenses help ensure a strong future for Minnesota's superb ski trail system.

Even during the coldest month of January, a jacket is often not needed while skiing in the Arrowhead.

Ski Country Regulations and Information Sources

So far, this chapter has dealt with subjects that pertain to cross country skiing, anywhere. Courtesy, safety, equipment and clothing are topics that are relevant to any skier, whether in Minnesota, Montana or Norway. The remainder of this chapter, however, addresses issues that are germane to skiing in the Arrowhead. Before gliding into Ski Country, familarize yourself with the state and federal regulations that apply and with sources of information that may be useful in planning and executing your trip.

STATE SKI LICENSES

Since the winter of 1984-85, the State of Minnesota has required all cross country skiers aged 16 - 64 who use any non-federal public trail designated and promoted for cross-country skiing to have ski licenses. The cost of the annual license is $5.00 for an individual and $7.50 for husband and wife. Skiers may, instead, purchase a daily permit for $1.00. The funds are used to maintain existing trails and to develop additional trail miles.

Daily permits are designed to be attached to the skier's outer clothing. The annual license consists of a card to be carried on the skier's person plus a sticker attached to one ski pole. Licenses are available from the License Bureau, Department of Natural Resources, 500 W. Lafayette Road, St. Paul, MN 55146. They can also be purchased at state parks or from over 200 agents statewide, including county auditors and chambers of commerce.

During the winter of 1984-85, $65,000 of state funds were allocated for trails in State Parks and Forests, while an additional $145,000 were distributed to over 70 clubs and communities statewide for Grant-in-Aid trails. That same winter, skiers purchased only 15,500 annual and 11,700 daily permits, generating $108,400. The DNR is authorized to spend only the amount raised by license sales during the preceding year. That resulted, unfortunately, in a 60% reduction in ski trail funding from 84-85 to 85-86.

Without the wholehearted support of cross-country skiers, the program is struggling. Many of the Arrowhead ski trails benefit from state funding — including many that fall entirely on National Forest lands.

PLEASE DO YOUR PART TO SUPPORT THE TRAILS on which you ski. Buy your license in the county where you do the most skiing, since state funds are appropriated according to the amount of revenue generated by each county. The $5 annual fee is a small price to pay for maintaining and expanding some of the best ski trails in America.

For more information, contact the DNR Trails and Waterways Unit, Box 52, D.N.R. Building, 500 Lafayette Road, St. Paul, MN 55146. Or phone (612) 296-6699.

The BWCAW.

THE BOUNDARY WATERS CANOE AREA WILDERNESS

The Boundary Waters Canoe Area Wilderness contains unlimited potential for cross country ski trips. Only a few of the designated ski trails included in this guide however, penetrate the wilderness area. Some of the Gunflint Lake area trails, the Banadad Trail, the South Farm Lake Trail and most of the trails originating from County Road 116 (the Echo Trail) between Ely and Crane Lake do enter the BWCAW. Skiers must be aware that most of the same regulations that apply to canoeists in summertime also apply to skiers. The only regulations that are suspended during the winter months are those dealing with permits and campsites. From October 1 through April 30, Travel Permits are NOT required for those visiting the Boundary Waters. And, unlike restrictions during the snow-free season, winter campers may camp anywhere and fires are not restricted to the Forest Service's fire grates. All other regulations, including the prohibition of nonburnable, disposable foods and beverage containers (cans and bottles), are in effect. Party size is always limited to no more than 10 people, and snowmobiles are prohibited in the wilderness, except at two locations approved by Federal law.

If you are planning to ski in the BWCA Wilderness, be sure that you are familiar with the rules and regulations that pertain to all visitors. For more information, contact Superior National Forest, U.S.D.A., P.O. Box 338, Duluth, Minnesota 55801.

For ideas on routes in the BWCAW that are not specifically designated as "ski trails," read the BOUNDARY WATERS CANOE AREA: Volume 1: The Western Region (Ely area) and Volume 2: The Eastern Region (Grand Marais and Tofte areas), Wilderness Press, 2440 Bancroft Way, Berkeley, CA 94704 or A PADDLER'S GUIDE TO THE BOUNDARY WATERS CANOE AREA, W.A. Fisher Company, Box 1107, Virginia, MN 55792-1107.

MAPS

Because most of the trails included in this book are "designated" by some governmental agency, civic organization or resort association as "official" ski trails, they have been mapped out in brochures, leaflets or one-page hand-outs that are available from the respective agencies, organizations or associations. All of the resorts along the Gunflint Trail and the North Shore, for instance, distribute their own maps to their guests. All of the state parks have standardized brochures that include maps along with other pertinent information about the parks. In the Ely, Crane Lake and Range areas, the Forest Service has done a good job distributing one-page hand-outs that illustrate the ski trails there. And so forth throughout the Arrowhead . . .

Inside the back cover of this book is a map of the entire Arrowhead region. It was designed to help you locate the ski trails and the resorts that cater to cross-country skiers.

Detailed maps of individual ski trails are **not** included in this guide. Unlike canoe routes and hiking trails, which are not likely to change significantly from one year to the next, ski trails can change frequently. Trails that are well-groomed this year may not be groomed at all next year. Indeed, a trail that was nicely groomed **last week** may be under a foot of unbroken snow **this** week, if a major storm happened along in between.

Every attempt has been made in this book to describe the ski trails as they **normally** appear. But the only way for you to get up-to-the-minute information about trail conditions is to drop by a local resort, ranger station or tourist information center. With few exceptions, maps are free, and the up-to-the-minute advisories are invaluable. The introduction to each ski trail tells where maps are available. You can have them sent to you in advance of your trip, or pick them up on the way to Ski Country.

Skiers who plan to make their own wilderness trails rather than use the marked trails of designated routes, should definitely carry good topographic maps. Study the topography of the area carefully **before** heading out. For the most part, the Northwoods forest is much too dense for off-trail, overland skiing. Skiers are restricted to unplowed logging roads and forest routes, hiking trails, portages, and the frozen surface of lakes and streams.

Regardless of the trails you choose, carry a good map and a reliable compass, and know how to use them both!

INFORMATION, PLEASE . . .

Following is a list of information sources that may be of interest to Arrowhead skiers.

For the latest information about **snow depth** at any of the ski areas in Minnesota, call the Minnesota Travel Information Center:

In the Twin Cities: (612) 296-5029

Toll-free in Minnesota: (800) 652-9747

Toll-free in the U.S.:   (800) 328-1461

For up-to-date **road conditions,** call the Minnesota Department of Transportation: (612) 296-3076

For **road emergencies** anywhere in Minnesota, call the Minnesota Highway Patrol: Dial "0" and ask the operator for "ZENITH 7000."

For **maps** of state ski trails, including State Parks, call the Minnesota Department of Natural Resources Outdoor Recreation Information Center:

In the Twin Cities: (612) 296-4776

Toll-free in Minnesota: (800) 652-9747

For those interested in **ice fishing,** fishing licenses can be obtained from the Department of Natural Resources License Center, 500 W. Lafayette Road, St. Paul, MN 55146.

WINTER CAMPING

Unbelievable as this may be to many folks, there is a growing number of camping enthusiasts who sincerely prefer winter over any other season in northern Minnesota. To them, summer is a crowded, buggy, noisy time of year. The northern Minnesota winter has no mosquitoes, no black flies, no biting gnats, no pesky black bears, no thunderstorms, no stifling humidity, and best of all, no other people around. In winter, one need not travel far on skis or snowshoes to enter a boreal wonderland of solitude — a pristine wilderness where the only tracks in the snow are those of deer, moose, wolves and snowshoe hares.

Millions of acres of government lands are available for winter exploration in the Arrowhead. Ageless canoe routes, seldom used hiking trails, abandonned logging roads and seasonal forest roads (not plowed in winter), as well as the designated ski trails described in this guide, provide campers with a virtually unlimited network of winter trails. But the Northwoods is no place for the inexperienced winter camper to strike out on his own.

Although this book offers valuable tips to the recreationalist, it is, by no means, intended to be a winter camping primer. For a good, sound introduction to this activity, read the books of two men who are experts in winter camping — both of whom live on the edge of the Boundary Waters Canoe Area Wilderness:

Cary, Bob: WINTER CAMPING. Brattleboro, Vermont: The Stephen Greene Press, 1979.

Drabik, Harry: THE SPIRIT OF WINTER CAMPING. Minneapolis: Nodin Press, 1985.

Winter camping in northern Minnesota requires special techniques, special gear and special clothing. More important than at any other time of year, the first-time camper should seek the guidance of someone with experience. If you have no friends to call on for assistance (indeed, if your friends think you are insane for even considering the prospect!), you might want to contact one of the organizations that specializes in winter camping instruction and/or survival techniques. In Minneapolis and St. Paul, local chapters of the American Lung Association conduct annual treks to the BWCA Wilderness. No prior skiing or camping experience is necessary. The programs are designed to raise money for the Lung Association, as well as to provide basic winter camping instruction for beginners. In the Ely area, three non-profit organizations have attracted national attention for their wilderness programs. Charles L. Sommers Wilderness Canoe Base conducts a winter camping program, called OKPIK, as part of the High Adventure Program of the Boy Scouts of America. Likewise, YMCA Camp Widjiwagan and Voyageur Outward Bound have winter camping programs. In addition, there are several outfitting companies on the perimeter of the BWCA Wilderness that specialize in winter recreational activities, including snowshoeing, dogsledding and cross country ski camping. Contact the Crane Lake Commercial Club, the Ely Chamber of Commerce and the Tip of the Arrowhead Association (Grand Marais) for information about winter camping outfitters.

For skiers who like to make their own tracks, the BWCA Wilderness offers countless trails across frozen lake surfaces — the same routes used by canoeists in summer.

CHAPTER 4

THE NORTH SHORE

It is a paradox. Buried deep within the heart of the upper midwest, 1500 miles from the nearest ocean, is one of the most beautiful "seashores" in North America. Minnesotans refer to it simply as the North Shore — that narrow 150-mile stretch of rugged real estate that borders the northwest shore of Lake Superior.

Created by volcanic activity through a long rift in the earth's crust millions of years ago and scoured by glaciers that last receded 10,000 years ago, the North Shore still displays the vestiges of a bona fide mountain range. Cartographers and geologists refer to the range as the Sawtooth Mountains. Locals just call it the North Shore Mountains. Regardless, it is here that some of the best cross country ski trails in the nation are found. They wind in and out of the Sawtooth Mountains, sometimes at lake level (602 feet above sea level), sometimes climbing to more than 1000 feet above the lake. Panoramas are breathtaking. Downhill runs are thrilling. The scenery is spectacular.

Currently there are 285 miles of ski trails along the North Shore, and an additional 125 miles of trails at short distances inland (Gunflint Trail Area and Heart of the Arrowhead region). Most of the trails have been developed for skiers only during the past few years. The future appears to hold even brighter prospects, with plans currently underway to join the North Shore Mountains trails with a contiguous network in the Finland Area (Heart of the Arrowhead Region).

Small population centers are nestled close to the shore of Lake Superior, scattered at frequent intervals between Duluth and the Canadian border. Some are so small, you might not recognize them as towns, were it not for the road-side signs. Traveling northeast from Duluth, the largest villages in geographic sequence are Two Harbors, Silver Bay, and Grand Marais. The smaller towns of Little Marais, Schroeder, Tofte and Lutsen are sandwiched between Silver Bay and Grand Marais. Grand Portage is situated near the very tip of the Arrowhead, only five miles from the Canadian border. These North Shore villages harbor most of the population of Lake and Cook counties. Motels, resorts, restaurants and service stations are scattered along the shoreline, providing ample accommodations for winter guests.

Except for the Two Harbors City Trail, all of the ski trails fall into three general categories: state park trails, North Shore Mountain Ski Trail system, and the Grand Portage Reservation trails. They have been developed by the Department of Natural Resources, the U.S. Forest Service in cooperation with the Lutsen-Tofte Tourism Association, the Lutsen Mountain Corporation and the Grand Portage Reservation. Cross country skiers owe these organizations a debt of gratitude for the superb systems of trails that have emerged along the North Shore.

For general information about this area, contact the Lutsen-Tofte Tourism Association, Box 115, Lutsen, MN 55612, or the Tip of the Arrowhead Association, Grand Marais, MN 55604.

The North Shore of Lake Superior is one of the most beautiful "seashores" in North America.

Two Harbors City Trail

Use Level: Moderate

Trail Type: Machine groomed and track-set

Difficulty: Mostly beginner; some advanced loops

Trail Length: 6.5 miles

Maps: Posted at trailhead and most intersections

Highlights: Good course for inexperienced skiers

Trailhead: On the east side of County Highway 2, one mile north of Highway 61 in Two Harbors. Large parking area available.

Description: Probably few people outside of Two Harbors are aware of this nice little trail system. It consists of a maze of interconnected loops in a mixed forest dominated by paper birch and aspen, along with some spruce, fir and cedar.

The trails are well groomed and single-tracked, and most intersections are marked with "you are here" maps. Most of the loops are on level to gently sloping terrain — ideal for inexperienced skiers and others with no propensity for downhill runs and uphill climbs. The largest loop, however, is cleverly designed in such a way that allows more experienced skiers to leave the main trail on short extension loops that offer more of a challenge. These are one-way loops that require intermediate to advanced skiing skills. Beginning skiers may simply stay on the main trail to avoid the more difficult challenges.

Since this is a Grant-in-Aid Trail for which state funds were allocated, state ski licenses are required for visitors. Competent skiers should have no difficulty skiing the entire course in an hour and a half or less.

FOR MORE INFORMATION: Contact Leon Hudson, 509 15th Avenue, Two Harbors, MN 55616. Or call (218) 834-2689.

The Two Harbors City Trail provides a network of easy trails through a beautiful forest of birch and aspen.

STATE PARKS
OF THE NORTH SHORE

The State of Minnesota has seen to it that the most scenic of the natural features along the North Shore will always be preserved for public recreation and buffered from economic development by including them in seven state parks. Six of these parks have trails for cross country skiers: Gooseberry Falls, Split Rock Lighthouse, Tettegouche, George H. Crosby Manitou, Temperance River and Cascade River state parks.

At all state parks in Minnesota, park permits are required for vehicles entering the parks. Daily ($3) or annual ($15) permits may be purchased at any of the park headquarters. Or they may be secured in advance from the Department of Natural Resources, Division of Parks and Recreation, Information Center, Box 40, 500 Lafayette Road, St. Paul, MN 55146. These permits go on sale November 1 for the following year, which allows skiers to enjoy an entire season with the purchase of only one permit. Park brochures with maps and descriptive information about each park may also be acquired at the state office. Questions may be channeled through a toll free number from anywhere in Minnesota: 1-800-652-9747.

State Ski Touring Licenses are also required at the parks. These permits are mandatory for skiers using state funded ski trails. They, too, may be purchased at the individual park headquarters or from the state office of the Division of Parks and Recreation.

Lunch break at an intersection in the North Shore Mountain Trail System.

44

Gooseberry Falls State Park

Use Level: Heavy

Trail Type: Machine groomed and track-set

Difficulty: Beginner through Advanced

Trail Length: 14½ miles

Maps: Brochure with map available from Park Manager

Highlights: Five waterfalls, Lake Superior overlooks

Trailhead: Adjacent to Highway 61, 12 miles northeast of Two Harbors. Parking areas are on both sides of the river, next to the highway.

Description: Because of its proximity to Duluth, Gooseberry Falls State Park has the most heavily used ski trails of any on the North Shore. Even on weekdays during the prime skiing months, the park will usually have visitors. And on weekends, it could be downright crowded at times.

Nevertheless, the outstanding scenery and the excellent variety of ski trails combine to make this state park one of the most interesting destinations in the Arrowhead. All of the trails are groomed and track-set. Although there are a number of challenging trail segments for advanced skiers, there is also a section of the park designed for beginners. Most of the trail system is suitable for intermediate skiers.

The highlight of this State Park is a series of five waterfalls along the Gooseberry River, which enters the park at the northwest corner and slashes southeast to the rocky shore of Lake Superior. Fortunately for sightseers and novice skiers, the best waterfalls are at the Highway 61 bridge, where Upper Falls and Lower Falls cascade a total of 170 feet before swirling into Lake Superior.

Located in the interior of the park's 1,662 acres is a deer yard where many white-tailed deer congregate to survive the harsh winters. Timber wolves are usually close by. Alert and quiet skiers may have an opportunity to see either of these beautiful animals.

Winter camping is allowed in the park's campgrounds, where campers have access to a shelter, drinking water and pit toilets. Free firewood and garbage pick-up is provided. Campers must backpack about ¾ mile from the park entrance to the grounds, register with the Park Ranger and pay a reduced winter camping fee.

Essentially, there are three trailheads for skiers using this park: one on either side of the Highway 61 bridge, adjacent to the river, and one at the entrance to the campground. The latter provides access to trails on the lakeside of the highway, where all of the trails (about 4 miles) were designed for novice skiers. Most of the trails here follow roadways that wind in and out of the campground area, near the shore of Lake Superior.

The trails on the inland side of Highway 61, on the other hand, are probably too difficult for most beginners. Advanced beginners and intermediates, however, may enjoy the more difficult trails along the southwest side of the Gooseberry River — a total round-trip distance of just over 3 miles. The trail climbs 220 feet and permits panoramic views from three overlooks. All of the loop is rated "Intermediate."

The most extensive network of trails is on the northeast side of the river. Most of it is suitable for intermediate skiers, but there are several advanced sections (2.3 miles in all) that are recommended for experts. The network begins at the Interpretive Center, and there are numerous loops available, including one that offers access to a good view of Fifth Falls. Near the north end of the trail system is a scenic overlook at a trail shelter, 200 feet above the Interpretive Center and 360 feet above Lake Superior. Four more overlooks are found in the eastern part of the Park.

FOR MORE INFORMATION: contact the Park Manager, Gooseberry Falls State Park, E. Star Route, Two Harbors, MN 55616. Or phone (218) 834-3855 for current snow conditions.

A spectacular chain of falls at Gooseberry Falls State Park is frozen over in mid-winter, but "opens up" during the March thaw.

Split Rock Lighthouse State Park

Use Level: Moderate

Trail Type: Machine groomed and track-set

Difficulty: Mostly intermediate or less

Trail Length: 6 miles

Maps: Brochure with map available from Park Manager

Highlights: Splitrock Lighthouse, good lakeshore trails, groomed and track-set.

Trailhead: At the parking lot adjacent to the lighthouse, 1/3 mile south of Highway 61, 20 miles northeast of Two Harbors.

Description: Splitrock Lighthouse is one of the most unique parks in Minnesota. A state park only since 1967, the lighthouse has been operated by the Minnesota Historical Society since 1976 as a sub-unit within the park. The Society will be opening a new visitors' center in the spring of 1986. Constructed in 1909 and 1910, after two tragic shipwrecks made it necessary, this historic site includes a lighthouse, a fog signal building, and oil storage house, and three stone residences. Other historic sites within the 2,042 acre park include a small abandoned fishing village at Little Two Harbors, an abandoned rock quarry and an old logging site at the mouth of the Split Rock River.

To cross-country skiers, however, the most impressive features of the park are probably the natural ones. The magnificent bluffs on which the lighthouse sits are easily viewed from good trails that parallel Lake Superior's rugged shoreline. These towering rock formations are the result of ancient volcanic activity, followed by twisting, compressing, uplifting and scouring — all of which resulted in a natural sculpture that surpasses anything a mortal artist could create.

A deer yard exists in the interior of the park, where white-tailed deer group together during the long winter months, amidst the forests of birch, ash, spruce and balsam fir.

Splitrock Lighthouse is one of the most unique state parks in Minnesota.

Opening by the winter of 1986-87 is a new Trail Center building — a heated facility that will have flush toilets, a warming area, exhibits about the park and trail information, as well as two sheltered outdoor fireplaces. It will serve as the focal point of the trail system.

The new Trail Center building at Splitrock has modern toilets, an indoor lounge area with wood stove and sheltered outdoor fireplaces.

The **LITTLE TWO HARBORS TRAIL** (1.6 miles) begins at the lighthouse, 130 feet above Lake Superior, and quickly descends 110 feet to follow the shoreline past the picnic area and campground. Along the way are some excellent views of the lighthouse and the rocky Lake Superior shoreline. It then leads away from the lake and intersects a large loop that is bisected by Highway 61.

The **MERRILL LOGGING TRAIL** (2.8 miles) constitutes the northern part of the loop. It follows a small creek to the northern border of the park, crosses the creek, and then loops toward the south, following old railroad logging grades. For more experienced skiers, the trail climbs to a scenic overlook 300 feet above the lake, where a shelter is located. Less experienced skiers can bypass the steep hill via a shorter route that rejoins the steeper trail after the most precipitous plunge. Use caution as the trail descends to cross Highway 61.

The **CORUNDUM MINE TRAIL** (1.6 miles) then continues the loop by following the Lake Superior shoreline from the Split Rock River back to Day's Hill. Several scenic points of view are passed along the way.

FOR MORE INFORMATION: Contact the Split Rock Lighthouse Park Manager, 1300 Hwy 61 East, Two Harbors, MN 55616. Or phone (218) 226-3065 for current snow conditions.

A splendid trail parallels the scenic North Shore of Lake Superior at Splitrock Lighthouse State Park.

Cold weather doesn't slow the work of woodpeckers in the Arrowhead.

The Baptism River enters Lake Superior at Tettegouche State Park.

Tettegouche State Park

Use Level: Light

Trail Type: 3 miles groomed and tracked for skiers: remainder not groomed or tracked.

Difficulty: Intermediate and Advanced

Trail Length: 12 miles

Connects to: Northwoods Ski Trail

Maps: Brochure with map available from Park Manager

Highlights: Highest falls within the state.

Trailhead: At the Baptism River Rest Area, adjacent to Highway 61, 4½ miles northeast of Silver Bay.

Description: Established on June 29, 1979. Tettegouche is Minnesota's newest state park. Its 4,650 acres contain a unique combination of natural features, including Lake Superior shoreline, rugged "mountainous" terrain, four inland lakes, the lower part of the Baptism River, the state's highest waterfall (80′ High Falls) and a lovely example of a northern hardwood forest. Half of the park is forested with aspen and birch, but large areas in the west-central part of the park are dominated by mature stands of sugar maple, yellow birch, basswood and white spruce.

White-tailed deer are among the most common of the 40 species of mammals known to inhabit the park. Moose, red fox, red squirrels and snowshoe hares are also seen. Skiers may even have an opportunity to view the timber wolf, though sightings are rare.

The Sawtooth Mountains rise to 1000 feet above Lake Superior, affording visitors outstanding views across the lake. On a clear day from atop Mt. Baldy, in fact, one may see as far as the Apostle Islands in Wisconsin.

Tettegouche is also rich in cultural features. Tettegouche Camp, on the west shore of Mic Mac Lake, was once the site of an Alger-Smith lumbering camp. At the turn of this century, loggers cut most of the Norway pine and white pine that had dominated the landscape there. A complex of rustic log buildings may still be seen at that site.

By the winter of 1986-87, a new information center, staffed with State Park employees, will be located at the winterized rest area adjacent to Highway 61. It will be a day-use area. But in 1987 a campground is scheduled to open.

Ski touring trails are expected to open for the first time during the winter of 1985-86. In past years, skiers followed hiking trails that were not groomed, nor set with tracks. Many of these trails are still not scheduled to be groomed, including the Mt. Baldy, Sawtooth Mountain and High Falls trails. Nevertheless, the main corridor trail connecting the trailhead at Highway 61 with the interior lakes and Tettegouche Camp *is* scheduled for grooming.

From the Baptism River rest area, adjacent to the highway, the **Nipisiquit Trail** first climbs gently from the shore of Lake Superior. Extensive stands of paper birch and aspen dominate the hillsides overlooking the big lake. As you approach the inland lakes, however, the forestation changes to that of mature sugar maple, yellow birch, basswood and white spruce. This intermediate trail extends 4 miles to the Tettegouche Valley and camp, 300 feet above the trailhead. A picnic area near the east end of Nipisiquit Lake hosts the junction of the southbound return route of the Nipisiquit Trail and the beginning of the **Tettegouche Camp Trail,** which continues westbound and skirts the west shores of Nipisiquit and Mic Mac lakes.

At Tettegouche Camp, the **Mt. Baldy Trail** leads northwest to a scenic overlook. This trail is **not** groomed for skiers. From near the summit of Mt. Baldy, the **Sawtooth Mountain Trail,** which is also not groomed, veers off to the south and loops back to Tettegouche Camp via the south side of Tettegouche Lake. This is a trail for experts. Several overlooks afford beautiful views of Tettegouche Lake, Lax Lake and Cedar Lake. Along the way, be alert to many sharp turns and hills. Near the Lax Lake overlook, a trail toward the west connects with Sawtooth Mountain Lodge, on the shore of Lax Lake.

Near the south end of Mic Mac Lake, a southbound trail leads out of the park. It connects the Tettegouche State Park trails with the Northwoods Ski Trail (See page 123).

FOR MORE INFORMATION: contact Tettegouche State Park Manager, 301 Lax Lake Road, Silver Bay, MN 55614. Or call (218) 353-7386 for current snow conditions.

Scenic views of Lake Superior are possible from numerous vantage points along the North Shore Mountain Trail.

George H. Crosby Manitou State Park

Use Level: Very Light

Trail Type: Natural environment trails, not groomed and track-set

Difficulty: Intermediate and Advanced

Trail Length: 6 miles

Maps: Brochure with map available from Park Manager

Highlights: Virgin pine and yellow birch: few people; rugged terrain

Trailhead: From State Highway 1 in Finland, drive northeast on County Road 7 for 7.6 miles to the park entrance. The parking area is .2 mile east of Co. Rd. 7. All of the drive except the 1.3 miles closest to Finland is on gravel roads.

Description: Crosby Manitou State Park is a secret! Located off the beaten path — the only one of the North Shore state parks with trails that are not accessible from Highway 61 — this wild and scenic park entertains only about 200 skiers each winter. Some of the other North Shore parks may see that many people on a given weekend. It's also the only park that doesn't groom its trails, and has no plans to do so (though in the past they have been packed to make a good base). What this all adds up to is a unique, wilderness experience for ambitious skiers who prefer to get away from the crowds.

The trails are narrow and hilly, and most of them are suggested for advanced skiers. Minnesota's North Shore Highlands is the closest thing to mountains in the midwest. Wooded peaks rise more than 800 feet above Lake Superior, which borders the southeast corner of the park. Unlike most of the surrounding forests, much of the park was never logged. As a result, skiers may glide through the oldest stand of yellow birch trees in Minnesota. There are also many old pines.

The Manitou River enters the northwest corner of the park and rushes toward its rendezvous with Lake Superior at the park's southeast corner. Along its course are 16 primitive campsites that are available only to those ambitious enough to hike, snowshoe or cross-country ski to them. Winter campers should be ready for rugged trails.

The prime wildlife attractions in the park are white-tailed deer, timber wolves and moose. Black bears roam throughout the park during the summer months, but skiers aren't likely to encounter any of these winter sleepers. A mid-winter confrontation would be a rare treat!

All trails begin at the parking lot, just east of the Ranger's cabin. **Middle Trail,** for intermediate skiers, leads northeast from the parking area for 1 kilometer to the Manitou River, where it connects with the West Manitou River Hiking Trail. This long hiking trail parallels the Manitou River and provides access to the many campsites distributed along its course. However it is **not** part of the recommended ski trail system.

South of the parking lot is a system of trails that is recommended for advanced and expert skiers — the **Yellow Birch Trail,** the **Cedar Ridge Trail,** the **Beaver Bog Trail** and the **Sidewinder Trail.** These rugged trails combine to form two large loops that reach to the southern perimeter of the park where deer yard in the winter. There are some terrific runs on the Yellow Birch, Cedar Ridge and Sidewinder trails. Closest to the parking lot, a 1.2 kilometer loop circumnavigates Benson Lake, where five more primitive campsites are located.

FOR MORE INFORMATION: Contact the Park Ranger, Crosby Manitou State Park, Box 482, Finland, MN 55603. There is no phone at the park, which is not staffed from December 1 through March 31.

A sign at the entrance to Crosby Manitou State Park reminds visitors that State Park Vehicle Permits are required, as at all state parks.

Temperance River State Park

Use Level: Moderate (Heavy some weekends)

Trail Type: Machine groomed and track-set

Difficulty: Beginner through Advanced

Trail Length: 7.5 miles

Connects To: North Shore Mountains Ski Trail system via the Lynx Trail

Maps: Brochure with map available from Park Manager; or Map #1 of the North Shore Mountains Ski Trail, available from the Lutsen-Tofte Tourism Association.

Highlights: Temperance River Gorge

Trailhead: On the northwest side of Highway 61, at the Temperance River bridge, one mile northeast of Schroeder. Another parking area and trailhead, more suitable for novice skiers, is located ¼ mile north of Schroeder, via a gravel road that begins at the gasoline station in Schroeder.

Description: Although most of this trail system is outside of the park boundaries, it is maintained by the Minnesota Parks Division. There is no fee for use of the trails. A variety of trails are available for all levels of skiers, beginner to advanced, utilizing three loops that extend into Superior National Forest and the Cross River Wayside area.

Unfortunately, with the trails sitting so close to Lake Superior, the skiing season is normally much shorter than for the trails sitting at higher elevations away from the lake. Seldom are the trails in good condition prior to Christmas or after the middle of March.

Typical of the hills bordering the North Shore, the forest here is predominately white birch, mixed with aspen and spruce. A winter deer yard exists in the area, and sightings of white-tailed deer are not uncommon. A silent skier might also be fortunate to view a timber wolf.

Three trail loops offer good alternatives for beginners, intermediate skiers and experts. All three loops provide skiers with a good blend of uphill, downhill and nearly level terrain. The steepness and length of slopes, however, vary considerably from one loop to another.

CROSS RIVER LOWER LOOP — 1.5 miles: This trail is designed for inexperienced skiers. Starting at the parking lot straight north of Schroeder, the trail is well marked and located on gentle grades. At the intersection of the Upper and Lower Cross River Loops is a sheltered bench for rest stops.

The parking lot access for the Lower Cross River Loop is also used for the Northshore Snowmobile Trail. Since the snowmobiles use a completely separate trail, however, skiers will encounter the machines only at the parking lot.

CROSS RIVER UPPER LOOP — 4 miles: Beginning at the Temperance River parking lot, this intermediate trail first climbs steadily uphill to an intersection with the Temperance River Road, about ½ mile from the parking lot. It crosses the road and then veers southwest and leads to a rest shelter overlooking the Cross River valley. After paralleling the river for a short distance, the trail then turns east for the return trip. At the intersection of the Upper and Lower Cross River Loops, follow the trail that is marked "Sawmill" and this will lead you to the Temperance River Road. As you follow the road north, you may share it with snowmobiles. It is the only part of the Temperance River trail system that is shared by skiers and snowmobiles, but this occurence is rare. The final ½ mile is the reverse of the first — but this time downhill!

TEMPERANCE RIVER TRAIL — 2 miles: This expert-rated trail begins on the west side of the Temperance River, and, at the beginning, it shares the same path as that used for the Upper Cross River Loop. After ½ kilometer of steady climbing, however, this trail crosses the river and begins its counterclockwise loop along the steep ravine that was once the riverbed of the Temperance. As you cross the steep ravine, you may have to "herring bone" up the other side. After following the course of the canyon, the trail follows a long downhill grade to the Temperance River and then parallels the river back to the crossing point. This is the most scenic of the three loops, but not suitable for inexperienced skiers.

At the northeast corner of the Temperance River Loop is a junction with the Lynx Trail, which is the southwestern most stretch of the North Shore Mountains Ski Trail, connecting the state park trails to the Sugar Bush system. (See the LYNX TRAIL on page 64.)

FOR MORE INFORMATION: Contact the Park Manager, Temperance River State Park, Box 33, Schroeder, MN 55613.

Temperance River State Park is the southwest anchor of the North Shore Mountains Ski Trail.

The Cross River plunges into Lake Superior at the
Cross River Wayside, in Schroeder.

A wooden bridge across the Cascade River affords skiers a spectacular view of the frozen falls in the dark canyon below.

Long downhill runs are characteristic of the Cascade River Trail system.

Cascade River State Park

Use Level: Moderate (Heavy some weekends)

Trail Type: Machine groomed and track-set

Difficulty: Beginner through Advanced

Trail Length: 13 miles (+ access to 27 adjoining miles)

Connects to: Cascade River and Deeryard Lake trails, and North Shore Mountain Ski Trail system

Maps: Brochure with map available from Park Ranger; or Map #5 of the North Shore Mountain Ski Trail, available from the Lutsen-Tofte Tourism Association.

Highlights: Excellent variety of trails, Sawtooth Mountain vistas, Cascade River and falls, bountiful wildlife.

Trailhead: The State Park entrance road is on the north side of Highway 61, 21 miles northeast of Tofte, 7½ miles northeast of Lutsen.

Description: The state park trails are part of one of the most extensive, oldest and best ski touring trail systems in the Arrowhead region. Along with the Cascade River and Deeryard Lake trails sitting northwest of the state park, the entire system offers skiers more than 40 miles of groomed trails for all levels of skiing. With 2,813 acres of beautiful North Shore terrain, Cascade River State Park alone boasts 13 miles of groomed trails through a diversity of natural settings. From the rugged Lake Superior shoreline to the towering heights of the Sawtooth Mountains, any skier should find trails that are both interesting and suitable to his skill level. The easiest trails parallel the lakeshore, while the most challenging trails lead to some breathtaking overlooks. Experts will find plenty of exciting downhill runs. And wildlife enthusiasts may ski inland to the largest winter deer yard in Minnesota.

For beginning skiers, the easiest trails form two loops that cover much of the park east of the Cascade River. From the parking lot, you may first glide through the campground en route to the river and then parallel the cascading stream as you climb steadily uphill. At the northern boundary of the park, you will then begin a long, gentle downhill run to Highway 61. After crossing the road, you'll return to the parking lot on a route that closely parallels Lake Superior, before it climbs up and crosses the highway again.

More advanced skiers may penetrate deeper inland to higher elevations. Moose Mountain offers a panoramic view from 500 feet above Lake Superior. A shelter house is located there, as well as at four other locations within the park. Anyone less than expert may find the final half mile to the summit tough going. But experts will enjoy the fast runs back down the mountain. Intermediate skiers have a number of options available to them.

The North Shore Mountains Ski Trail leads north from the Moose Mountain trail, at a junction ½ mile from the summit. At the other end of the system, a trail crosses the Cascade River, affording a beautiful view of the falls below, and then joins up with the Cascade River Trails which lead north to the Deer Yard Trails (See page 79 for more information about these trails.) The North Shore Mountains Ski Trail exits the park at the southwest corner and leads to the Solbakken trails.

Because of their proximity to Lake Superior, the ski trails closest to Highway 61 may not have as much snow cover as those sitting at higher elevations away from the lake. Seldom are the lakeside trails in good condition prior to Christmas or after mid-March, while the inland trails generally offer extended seasons.

FOR MORE INFORMATION: Contact the Park Manager, Cascade State Park, Lutsen, MN 55612. Or phone (218) 387-1543 for current snow conditions.

The largest deer yard in Minnesota is found near Cascade River State Park.

NORTH SHORE MOUNTAINS SKI TRAIL

Use Level: Moderate

Trail Type: Machine groomed and track-set

Difficulty: Abundance of trails for all skill levels

Trail Length: 126 miles

Connects to: Temperance River State Park, Sugar Bush Trails, Moose Fence Trails, Oberg Mountain Trail, Lutsen Ski Touring Trails, Lutsen Mountain Norpine System, Solbakken Trails, Cascade State Park, Cascade River and Deeryard Lake Trails, and the Bally Creek Trails.

Maps: Maps #1, 2, 3, 4 & 5 of the North Shore Mountains Ski Trail, available from the Lutsen-Tofte Tourism Association

Highlights: The longest continuous system of groomed and tracked ski trails in Minnesota; splendid opportunities for "norpine" skiing; long season; good snow depths; outstanding panoramas of Lake Superior and the rugged Sawtooth Mountains; Lodge-to-Lodge ski-through trips available.

Trailhead: Paralleling Highway 61 for 22 miles along Lake Superior's North Shore, there are numerous good accesses to this trail system from Schroeder on the southwest end to Bally Creek Road at the northeast end. In between are more than a dozen trailheads for skiers using the various loops that are joined by the North Shore Mountains Ski Trail.

Description: Many words could describe this extensive system of trails. Extraordinary. Spectacular. Superior. Exquisite. Take your pick. They all apply . . .

The trails wind along a 22-mile stretch of the scenic Lake Superior shoreline, sometimes closely following the shore, but more often

Accesses to the North Shore Mountain Trail are marked at several locations along Highway 61.

penetrating the interior highlands, as high as 1000 feet above the lake. The system is designed for the enjoyment of all types of skiers, beginners to advanced. After negotiating the incline from Lake Superior to the highlands, most of the trails follow gently rolling terrain. Intermediate skiers should find nearly all of the system suitable for their skill level, while beginners should be more selective in the trails they choose. There are some areas that provide a challenge for experts. By planning ahead, regardless of your skiing ability, you should be able to find miles of trails that will provide hours (if not days) of skiing pleasure.

The only part of the trail system where fees are charged is at Lutsen Mountain, where chair lifts are used by Norpine skiers. Though no fees are charged elsewhere, the State of Minnesota does require a cross-country ski license in the possession of skiers using parts of the system. They can be purchased at state park offices, the Lutsen Touring Center and at other locations along the North Shore.

Snow conditions are usually quite good and the season is long for most of the North Shore Mountains trail system. Along Lake Superior's coastline, however, the moderating effects of the lake are both a blessing and a curse. On the one hand, bitterly cold weather is rare near the shore, where the climate is tempered by the lake. But this effect also produces less than desirable skiing conditions during the early and late parts of the ski season. In contrast to the interior highlands, skiing near the coast is seldom good prior to Christmas or after the middle of March. Since most of the trail system lies a few miles inland and several hundred feet higher in elevation, however, the heavier snowfall and somewhat cooler temperatures assure excellent snow conditions, often into mid-April. What this all means to you is this: Don't be quick to pass judgement on the North Shore Mountains Ski Trail if you find an absence of snow or the presence of slush along the coast. Chances are good that, only a short distance inland, the trails will be fine from December at least through the end of March.

In addition to an excellent system of trails, the North Shore is also blessed with a fine group of four-season resorts that offer skiers an opportunity to ski from lodge to lodge. Skiers can make arrangements to ski from one end of the system to the other, with nights spent at various resorts along the way. Luggage is transported from one establishment to the next. All the skier must carry is a day pack with lunch and camera. This is one of the best ways to enjoy the whole North Shore experience. Your vacation should be spent skiing, dining and resting, not worring about shuttling cars and luggage from one point to another.

White-tailed deer abound along the North Shore.

A cedar-line access trail connects Highway 61
with the main corridor of the North Shore
Mountains Ski Trail.

The Trail

The North Shore Mountains Ski Trail is a network of 126 miles of ski trails anchored by several loops between the Temperance River at the southwest end and Bally Creek at the northeast end. In between are the Sugar Bush Trails, the Moose Fence Trail, the Oberg Mountain Trail, the Lutsen Ski Touring Trails, the Lutsen Mountains Norpine System, the Solbakken Ski Trails, the Deeryard Lake Trail and Cascade River Trails. All of these loops are discussed separately on the pages that follow. Each can be enjoyed separately, or different loops can be joined together by skiing on connecting trails that constitute the main "corridor" trail from one end of the system to the other. Following the trail from southwest to northeast, the network begins at **Temperance River State Park.** The **Lynx Trail** heads northeast towards Carlton Peak and joins Temperance River State Park with the **Sugar Bush Trails.** From the east side of the Homestead Loop, a connecting trail leads northeast over gently rolling terrain to the **Oberg Mountain Trail.** From the southeast end of the Oberg Mountain loop, the **Sea Villa Trail** leads south and drops gently downhill toward Lake Superior. The corridor trail branches off the Sea Villa Trail and continues in an easterly direction to join the **Lutsen Ski Touring Trails.** After crossing the Poplar River, the trail turns inland again and travels north and east to the **Solbakken Trails.** The corridor trail forms the bottom edge of the Massie and Hall loops as it continues over rolling landscape en route to the **Cascade River Ski Trails** and **Cascade River State Park.** Beyond the northernmost loop in the state park, near Moose Mountain, the trail no longer parallels Lake Superior's shoreline. It climbs north-northeast, crosses the Pike Lake Road and then terminates at **Bally Creek.**

The corridor trail, itself, is suitable for intermediate and advanced skiers, though parts of it can be enjoyed even by novice skiers. Beginners, however, are more likely to feel comfortable on some of the less demanding trails adjacent to the corridor.

Norpine Skiing

The North Shore Mountains Ski Trail is ideally suited to "Norpine skiing" — a combination of Nordic and Alpine skiing. At Lutsen Mountains Ski Area, the same chair lifts that carry Alpine skiers to the tops of the slopes also transport cross-country skiers to the beginnings of several Nordic trails that wind throughout the Lutsen Mountain highlands and then descend back to the base of the slopes. Lutsen Mountains rise over 1000 feet above Lake Superior, and it is possible to ski from the summit of the highest peak all the way down to the shore of Lake Superior. For those who prefer the excitement of downhill runs to the strain of uphill climbs, Norpine skiing may be just the "ticket."

But Lutsen isn't the only place where Norpine skiing may occur. Because there are several access roads leading inland to the elevated interior trails, it is possible to arrange transportation to those inland accesses and then ski back to Highway 61. Some resorts will shuttle their guests to various starting points that allow them to ski all day and end up back at the resorts. For a modest fee, Lutsen Touring Center will make arrangements to shuttle any skier to various starting points throughout the trail system. Following are a few Norpine route suggestions to consider:

— Begin at the Britton Peak parking lot, 2.8 miles up the Sawbill Trail from Highway 61 in Tofte, and ski southwest down the Lynx Trail to Temperance River State Park.

— Begin at the Britton Peak parking lot and ski east through the Sugar Bush trails and then southeast to one of several possible resorts along Highway 61 (Cobblestone Cabins, Chateaux Leveaux, Gull Harbor Condominiums or Best Western Cliff Dweller).

— Begin at the Moose Fence parking area, 7½ miles up the Sawbill Trail from Tofte, and ski southeast to the Oberg Mountain loop and then down the long, gently sloping Sea Villa Trail to Lutsen Sea Villas on Highway 61. Or continue east to Bailey's Corner or Lutsen Resort.

— Begin at the Oberg Mountain parking lot, 2.1 miles up the Onion River Road from Highway 61. After skiing the Oberg Mountain Loop, ski downhill to Lutsen Sea Villas, Bailey's Corner or Lutsen Resort.

— Begin at the Babineau Corner, on the Pike Lake Road (#45), and, after skiing the Deeryard Lake Trail, glide down the long runs leading to Cascade Lodge or Cascade River State Park on Highway 61.

— Begin at Bear Track's Bally Creek Camp, 6 miles northwest of Grand Marais, and ski southwest to Cascade Lodge or Cascade River State Park.

FOR MORE INFORMATION: Contact the Lutsen-Tofte Tourism Association, Box 115, Lutsen, MN 55612.

Deeryard Lake is a lovely destination for skiers.

The North Shore mountains afford panoramic vistas for skiers and winter photographers.

Sugarbush Ski Trails

Use Level: Moderate

Trail Type: Machine groomed and track-set

Difficulty: Beginner, Intermediate and Advanced

Trail Length: 25.6 miles

Connects To: North Shore Mountains Ski Trail, Oberg Mountain Trail, Moose Fence Trails, and the Lynx Trail to Temperance River State Park.

Maps: Map #2 of the North Shore Mountain Ski Trail, available from the Lutsen-Tofte Tourism Association.

Highlights: Excellent trails through an interesting variety of forest habitats.

Trailhead: From Highway 61 in Tofte, drive north on County Road #2 (Sawbill Trail) for 2.8 miles to the Britton Peak Parking Lot, on the east side of the road.

Description: The Sugarbush Ski Trail system is a beautiful assortment of groomed and track-set loops that meander throughout the higher elevations of the Sawtooth Mountains. Excellent loops of almost any length and difficulty can originate from the Britton Peak trailhead. The trails are well marked with blue diamonds, directional arrows, caution signs and "you are here" maps. To protect the set tracks and to avoid encountering unmarked caution hills, it is recommended that the directional arrows should be followed on the loops. The degree of difficulty is clearly marked at the beginning of each loop.

One of the best networks of trails along the North Shore, the system falls under the jurisdiction of the U.S. Forest Service, Tofte Ranger District, and is groomed by the Lutsen-Tofte Tourism Association.

Elegant stands of sugar maple and white birch dominate the hilly landscape, but some of the trails pass through cedar swamps and a mixture of conifers and aspen interspersed throughout the maple and birch. Numerous outstanding panoramas are possible from the hardwood-covered ridges.

Intermediate skiers should feel comfortable on most of the trail system, but there are some steep downhill runs that should thrill most experts, too. Novice skiers will find plenty of satisfaction on the "Piece of Cake" and "Woodduck" loops.

Access to all of the loops begins at the Britton Peak Parking Lot and follows a ½ mile trail over gently rolling terrain amidst an old stand of sugar maple trees. The trail loops around the base of Britton Peak. It is double-tracked for two-way traffic.

WOODDUCK LOOP (½ mile) and **PIECE OF CAKE LOOP** (.6 mile): The easiest of the five loops, these trails are easily negotiated by inexperienced skiers. The two loops pass over gentle slopes amidst maples interspersed with aspen and spruce. Peering through large maples, skiers may view Lake Superior and Carlton Peak to the southwest.

HOGBACK LOOP (2 miles): Recommended for intermediate skiers, this trail begins on the north side of the Piece of Cake Loop. Following the loop in a clockwise direction, skiers first climb to a ridge overlooking the Temperance River. At the north end of the loop, a short, steep climb is required to reach the top of a hogback ridge. A nice downhill run then leads back toward the east end of the Piece of Cake Loop.

BRIDGE LOOP (1¼ miles): Another route for intermediate skiers, the Bridge Loop begins on the south side of the Piece of Cake Loop, and then leads straight east. After a sharp curve toward the north, it descends on a long downhill slope and crosses the Springdale Creek bridge at the bottom. The remaining part of the loop is an uphill climb along the side of the creek. After a slight downhill curve through an old cedar swamp, there is a short, but steep incline back to the Piece of Cake Loop, at its east end.

HOMESTEAD LOOP (4.7 miles): The Homestead Loop offers intermediate skiers an extended tour across rolling hills of birch and aspen. Some birch trees, in fact, are extraordinarily large in this area. The trail first follows a rolling ridge along the southeast side of the loop. At the east end of the loop, near the trail's junction with the Picnic Loop (and North Shore Mountain Trail to Oberg Mountain), there is a steep downhill run that curves to the northwest. At that point, the trail begins a long, gradual ascent to a ridge overlooking the West Branch Onion River Valley. After passing over several small hills, the route enters a cedar swamp bordered by scenic cliffs on both sides. A short, steep climb brings you back to the Piece of Cake Loop. Follow it southeast to the trailhead, or, if there is time for more excitement, veer north on the Hogback Loop before heading back to Britton Peak.

PICNIC LOOP (15½ miles): This is one of the longest, most scenic, least used and most challenging ski touring trails in the North Shore Mountains system. It incorporates parts of the Hogback Loop, the Homestead Loop and the Oberg Mountain Trail (see page 70), and it begins on the same easy trails used by the Wooduck and Piece of Cake loops. The best way to follow the loop is in a clockwise direction, beginning at the northern tip of the Hogback Loop. From that point, the trail first drops steeply down into a cedar swamp bordered by cliffs, and then climbs more gradually to maple-covered ridges that afford nice vistas of the Temperance River valley and the West Branch Onion River valley.

At the north end of the loop, the trail is joined by a connecting route leading to the Moose Fence Trails. As the Picnic Loop veers toward the southeast, there is an excellent view of Oberg and LeVeaux Mountains. The trail then drops down to cross the Onion River and intersects with the Oberg Mountain Trail. Continuing south-southeast, the two loops share a double-tracked trail to the next intersection, where the Oberg Mountain Trail continues heading southeast to a parking lot and trailhead adjacent to the Onion River Road. This is another good access to the Picnic Loop, as well as to the Oberg Mountain Trail. The Picnic Loop leads southwest from the junction, crosses the West Branch Onion River, passes north of Leveaux Mountain, and then joins the east end of the Homestead Loop. A panoramic view of Oberg and Leveaux mountains is possible from an overlook near the top of an incline, where the trail makes a sharp bend toward the southeast. Near the west side of Leveaux Mountain is the junction with a trail from Lake Superior that provides access for guests at several resorts along the lake (Cobblestone Cabins, Chateau Leveaux, Gull Harbor Condominiums and Bestwestern Cliff Dweller Motel).

As the name of this loop might imply, it is long enough for most skiers to plan a picnic lunch. For tips on how to get the most enjoyment out of these trails, see the North Shore Mountains Ski Trail on page 61.

FOR MORE INFORMATION: Contact the Tofte Ranger District, United States Forest Service, Tofte, MN 55615. Or call (218) 663-7280 for current snow conditions.

Downhill runs that require extra caution are clearly marked on the Sugar Bush Trail system.

Intersections are well marked on the Sugarbush Trails with "you are here" signs.

A good bridge carries skiers across the Onion River, at the northeast corner of the Picnic Loop.

Some extraordinary birch trees grow along the Homestead Loop.

Excellent loops of almost any length and difficulty can originate from the Britton Peak trailhead.

Oberg Mountain Trail

Use Level: Moderate

Trail Type: Machine groomed and track-set

Difficulty: Mostly Intermediate; some Advanced

Trail Length: 7½ miles

Connects To: Picnic Loop and North Shore Mountains Ski Trail

Maps: Map #3 of the North Shore Mountains Ski Trail, available from the Lutsen-Tofte Tourism Association

Highlights: Excellent trails through scenic "mountains"

Trailhead: From Highway 61, 5 miles southwest of Lutsen (4½ miles northeast of Tofte), drive northwest on the Onion River Road (Forest Route 336) for 2.1 miles to the parking lot on the west side of the road. The road is not plowed beyond this point.

Description: Like its neighboring ski area to the west, the Sugar Bush Trails, the Oberg Mountain Trail provides skiers with a challenging route across a rolling landscape covered largely with a dense forest of sugar maple trees. The entire loop is north of Oberg Mountain, forming a large "circle" around Oberg Lake.

Skiers do NOT use the Oberg Hiking Trails, which hug the side of Oberg Mountain. The hiking trails are steep, narrow and not groomed for skiers. Sharp turns and "switch-backs" make the trails suitable only for expert skiers who prefer breaking trails and flirting with hazardous terrain. These trails begin on the east side of the Onion River Road, directly across from the parking lot turn-off.

The ski trail, on the other hand, parallels the hiking trail, closer to Oberg Lake, and it intersects the Onion River Road at a point 100 yards north of the parking lot turn-off.

The Oberg Mountain loop may be skied in either direction, but traveling in a clockwise direction is probably the most enjoyable. The trail begins at the northwest end of the parking lot and leads northwest to a junction with the Picnic Loop. The following 2 miles of double-tracked trail is shared by the users of both loops, as well as by "norpine" skiers starting their downhill journey at the Moose Fence trailhead. At the next junction, near the Onion River bridge, the Picnic Loop veers to the west, while the Oberg Mountain Trail heads northeast. After crossing the Onion River Road, the trail continues in an easterly direction, gradually climbing to an elevation 900 feet above Lake Superior on a slope covered with sugar maple. As the trail curves toward the south, there is a long gradual downhill run that drops more than 300 feet to an intersection with the North Shore Mountain Trail.

Norpine skiers may continue on the long, gentle downhill run all the way to Lake Superior, 600 feet below. But the Oberg Mountain Trail steers west from the junction and then passes over rolling hills en route to the Onion River Road and your origin at the parking lot. You'll see Oberg Lake on the North side of the trail as you approach the end of the loop.

Less experienced skiers may avoid the most difficult part of the loop — the westernmost stretch that is shared with the Picnic Loop — by skiing up the gentle grade of the Onion River Road, which is also groomed and double-tracked for skiers.

FOR MORE INFORMATION: Contact the Tofte Ranger District, United States Forest Service, Tofte, MN 55615. Or call (218) 663-7280 for current snow conditions.

A large map at the trailhead directs skiers to the Oberg Mountain Trail.

Moose Fence Trail

Use Level: Light

Trail Type: Mostly natural environment trails, not groomed and track-set

Difficulty: Intermediate, primarily

Trail Length: 4.8 miles

Connects to: Picnic Loop and North Shore Mountains Ski Trail

Maps: Map #2 of the North Shore Mountains Ski Trail, available from the Lutsen-Tofte Tourism Association.

Highlights: Lightly travelled trails that are not track-set.

Trailhead: From Highway 61 in Tofte, drive north on County Road #2 (the Sawbill Trail) for 7½ miles to a parking lot on the east side of the road.

Description: The Moose Fence Trail offers a variety of trail conditions through an interesting variety of forest habitat that receives very light use. It provides good warm-up loops for more advanced skiers or a half-day outing in itself for less experienced skiers. It is also an excellent starting point for "norpine" skiers who want to ski from an upland access down to Lake Superior, since the trail connects to the Picnic, Oberg Mountain and Sea Villa trails, with connecting trails to most of the North Shore resorts in this area. The main corridor route leading back toward Lake Superior is groomed and double-tracked across the northern part of the Maple Loop, but the southern half of the Maple Loop and all of the Upland Loop are not groomed and tracked. This gives skiers an opportunity to break trail after new snowfalls, and experience a feeling of wilderness exploration. Throughout the two loops, however, the trails are clearly marked (most of the time) with blue diamonds.

There are no facilities at the parking lot or along the trail, but the parking lot is regularly plowed. At the trailhead is a 10-acre fenced in research plot, where Forest Service researchers are trying to develop a strain of white pine that is genetically resistant to the blister rust disease. The trail gets its name from the fence that encircles the plot, designed to keep moose from munching on the young trees.

The Maple Loop passes through a young spruce plantation above Sixmile Creek.

72

This trail system is divided into two loops, with the groomed corridor trail running right down the middle, en route to the Picnic Loop (See page 68). The beginning ⅓ mile of the trail follows the fence line around the research plot. Although either direction is possible, there is a steep (though short) uphill climb on the south side of the plot. Circumnavigating the research plot in a clockwise direction requires a much more gradual ascent to the northeast corner of the plot. Soon after leaving the research area, you'll enter a stand of sugar maple trees and then glide down a gentle slope to cross a stream near the junction of the Maple Loop trail. At this point, you leave the nicely groomed trail behind and negotiate the **Maple Loop** (2½ miles) in a counter-clockwise direction. When snow cover is not too thick, fallen trees, stumps and rocks may create "moguls" on your path. After the trail winds through a stand of mature maples, it then enters a young spruce plantation on the slopes above Sixmile Creek. Watch carefully for the trail, as it is sometimes difficult to see in this open area, where the view across Sixmile Creek is lovely. The trail then enters a dense stand of conifers, where windfalls may obstruct the path. Don't give up! You're not lost! Soon the trail will once again join the good, wide corridor trail that leads west to the parking lot.

The **Upland Loop** (2 miles) intersects the northern part of the Maple Loop. It is a flat, easy trail that penetrates a newly forested area. Watch carefully for the trail in the open areas.

FOR MORE INFORMATION: Contact the Tofte Ranger District, United States Forest Service, Tofte, MN 55615. Or call (218) 663-7280 for current snow conditions.

The steepest part of the Moose Fence Trail is the short climb past the 10-acre research plot.

Lutsen Ski Touring Trails

Use Level: Moderate

Trail Type: Machine Groomed and Track-set

Difficulty: Beginner and Intermediate

Trail Length: 6 miles

Connects to: Lutsen Mountains Norpine System and the North Shore Mountains Ski Trail

Maps: Map #3 of the North Shore Mountains Ski Trail, available from the Lutsen-Tofte Tourism Association, and at the Lutsen Ski Touring Center.

Highlights: Scenic Poplar River

Trailhead: Across from Lutsen Resort on the north side of Highway 61, 7.3 miles northeast of Tofte.

Description: Lutsen Touring Center is a good source of information about the entire North Shore Mountains Ski Trail system and the Lutsen Mountains Norpine System. There you'll find sales and rental of cross-country gear, as well as maps, wax and refreshments. Outside the door are the beginnings of several small loops that offer skiers an opportunity to warm up and test their waxes, or to simply enjoy the scenic landscape along the lovely Poplar River.

Unfortunately, with the trails situated so close to Lake Superior, the ski season here may be truncated, due to the warming effects of the lake. Along the shore of Lake Superior, skiing seldom occurs before Christmas or after mid-March. At higher elevations a very short distance inland, however, the snow conditions are likely to be much better — and for a longer season.

Four short loops provide a quick introduction to ski touring along the North Shore. Two of the shortest loops, the **East Canyon Circle** and the **West Canyon Circle,** offer scenic views of the Poplar River, and they take only a few minutes to negotiate. The **Alderwood Round** and **Turnagain** trails begin at the old Lutsen stable, west of the Touring Center. Longer than the canyon loops, both offer good opportunities to test the waxes before heading out on longer routes.

Though the **Upper Blue Jay Circle** and **Lower Blue Jay Circle** are rated "intermediate," most of the trail is easy enough for inexperienced skiers. They both climb gentle slopes that are covered primarily with birch, spruce and maple trees. The immature growth provides good forage for a variety of wildlife. The northernmost point of the Upper Circle is 200' above the trailhead. The first half of the loop is nearly all uphill, while the second half is nearly all down. Other than a steep dip at the junction of the two loops, the trail is pretty tame. The North Shore Mountains Ski Trail intersects the west side of the Upper Blue Jay Circle.

The **River Trail** crosses a small bridge over the Poplar River and then leads north along the river's east side. The North Shore Mountains Ski Trail leading to Solbakken intersects the River Trail at an elevation 200 feet above the Touring Center.

The **Lodge Run,** on the other hand, parallels the Poplar River on the west side. It leads north to the Moose Mountain Trail, and access to the Lutsen Mountains Norpine System.

FOR MORE INFORMATION: Contact the Lutsen Ski Touring Center, Lutsen, MN 55612.

The Lutsen Ski Touring Center is a good source of information about the entire North Shore Mountains system.

A bridge allows skiers to cross the Poplar River near the Lutsen Ski Touring Center.

Lutsen Mountains Norpine System

Use Level: Moderate

Trail Type: Machine groomed and track-set

Difficulty: Trails for all skill levels, beginner through advanced.

Trail Length: 22 miles

Connects to: Lutsen Ski Touring Trails and North Shore Mountains Ski Trail

Maps: Available at the lift ticket office, Lutsen Mountains Corporation, or Map #3 of the North Shore Mountains Ski Trail

Fee: $5.00/day

Highlights: Chairlifts to the top of the Sawtooth Mountains enable mostly downhill skiing on well-groomed tracks.

Trailhead: The lift ticket office for Lutsen Mountains Corporation. From Highway 61, 7½ miles northeast of Tofte, drive north on County Road #36 for 2 miles to the Lutsen Mountain Ski Area.

Description: Lutsen offers skiers a unique combination of Nordic and Alpine skiing, called Norpine. Utilizing the chairlifts at the well-known downhill ski area, cross-country skiers have the luxury of skiing on well-groomed, double-tracked trails in the Sawtooth Mountain highlands WITHOUT having to climb the slopes. Miles of excellent trails lead deep into the backcountry of Superior National Forest at elevations nearly 1000 feet above Lake Superior. After penetrating the remote interior wilderness, skiers may then glide all the way down to the lake for food, rest and refreshment at one of the nicest lodges in Minnesota.

This is one of only two privately managed ski areas in the Arrowhead at which trail use fees are charged. But, then, for those skiers who prefer the fun of downhill runs over the drudgery of uphill climbs, the modest fee is well worth it. Ski passes may be obtained at the lift ticket office.

In contrast to the ski trails in the lakeside vicinity of the Lutsen Ski Touring Center, near Highway 61, these highland trails usually have an abundance of snow and the skiing season is longer.

Five excellent trails weave throughout the Lutsen Mountains. All are well-groomed and double-tracked to accommodate the influx of skiers on busy weekends.

The **Moose Mountain Trail** (6.2 miles) is strictly for experts. The journey begins with a chairlift to the summit of Moose Mountain, 600 feet higher than its base at the Poplar River. The trail winds along the top of the mountain in a southwesterly direction, where skiers may enjoy fine views of Superior National Forest and Lake Superior beyond. Then the trail loops sharply back toward the east and descends to the Poplar River Valley. En route, skiers must be alert for Alpine skiers, whose path is crossed on three different runs. Before reaching the bottom, skiers have the option to connect to the Mystery Mountain Trail or to return to the base of the chair lift.

The **Mystery Mountain Loops** (9.3 miles) are designed for intermediate skiers. This beautiful network of trails begins with a lift to the top of Mystery Mountain. Heading first in a westerly direction, the trail soon splits and offers skiers the option of descending on either side of the mountain. One route drops gradually down the north slope to intersect with the Ullr Mountain Loop. The other route allows skiers to glide through the valley between Mystery and Moose mountains, with options to join the Moose Mountain or Poplar River trails, or to continue back to the base of the lift.

The **Ullr Mountain Loop** (3.1 miles) is the only trail in the system rated for beginning skiers. A chair lift transports skiers to the top of Ullr Mountain, the lowest of the peaks surrounding the Lutsen ski area. The trail meanders throughout the Ullr highlands and then descends gradually to the Poplar River Valley. Following a ridge above the river, the trail returns to the Upper Parking Lot at the base of Ullr Mountain.

The **Eagle Mountain Trail** (1¼ miles) is a short route from the top of the Bridge Chair Lift. It loops first toward the east and then swings back toward the southwest as it drops over 500 feet to County Road 36 and its intersection with the Poplar River Valley Trails.

The **Poplar River Valley Trails** (1.9 miles) are the "connecting links" for the ski area. Skiers leaving from the Village Chalet can ski downhill to the base of Moose Mountain for a lift to the summit of the Moose Trail. Or they can follow the Poplar River up to the Poma Lift at the base of Mystery Mountain. Residents and guests leaving the townhouse area at Lutsen Mountain Village may also acquire access to all of the ski lifts by using the River trails, which are considered intermediate level trails.

FOR MORE INFORMATION: Contact Lutsen Mountain Ski Area, Lutsen, MN 55612. Or call (218) 663-7281.

Solbakken Ski Trails

Use Level: Moderate to Light

Trail Type: Machine groomed and track-set

Difficulty: Mostly intermediate

Trail Length: 8 miles

Connects To: North Shore Mountains Ski Trail

Maps: Map #4 of the North Shore Mountains Ski Trail, available from the Lutsen-Tofte Tourism Association

Highlights: Deer wintering area. Variety of forest habitats

Trailhead: Solbakken Resort, 1¼ miles northeast of the town of Lutsen on Highway 61. Trail access and parking are also available along the "Hall Road." From Highway 61, .9 mile northeast of Solbakken Resort, turn north onto County Road 41 and drive .4 mile uphill to the North Shore Mountains Ski Trail.

Description: Four trails are accessible from the Solbakken trailhead: two very short loops near the coast of Lake Superior and two longer loops that climb to higher elevations where two old homesteads rest. Three of the four trails are recommended for intermediate skiers, while one is easy enough for beginners to enjoy.

White-tailed deer are frequently seen in this area, where stands of cedar — their favorite winter munchies — are common. Astute observers of wildlife might also see signs of timber and "brush" wolves, fox, snowshoe hare and a variety of birds and rodents.

Skiing up the access trail from Highway 61 at Solbakken Resort, skiers quickly reach the first small loop — **Deer Tracks Loop** (1/2 mile). This is the easiest trail that beginners should enjoy, one that circles through a forest of cedar where deer are known to winter.

The **Whiteside Loop** (1/2 mile) is only slightly longer than the Deer Track Loop, but more difficult. Skied in a clockwise direction, much of the trail descends gradually, while the lower part of the loop is nearly level. The only difficult part of the loop is one short steep section in the upper left corner.

A northbound access trail from the top of the Whiteside Loop crosses Jonvick Creek and climbs to an intersection with the North Shore Mountains Trail, which constitutes the southern parts of the Massie and Hall loops.

The **Massie Loop** (3.4 miles), a trail for intermediate skiers, continues climbing, steeply at times, to the Massie Homestead, an old abandoned farm that sits on private property. The trail then levels off as it swings toward the east and leads to an intersection with the Hall Loop. At that point, skiers may shoot down the fast "North Star Run" to the bottom of the loop.

Or they may join the **Hall Loop** (3.2 miles). This trail climbs to a high ridge overlooking Lake Superior, 500 feet above the trailhead. From there it is a long, gentle downhill glide to an intersection with the North Shore Mountains Trail. An eastbound trek over rolling terrain brings skiers to the parking area at County Road 41 (the Hall Road) and eventually to the access trail leading south to Solbakken Resort. Like the Massie Loop, part of the Hall Loop crosses private property. Treat it with respect.

FOR MORE INFORMATION: Contact Solbakken Resort, East Star Route Box 170, Lutsen, MN 55612.

Cascade River and Deeryard Lake Trails

Use Level: Moderate

Trail Type: Machine groomed and track-set

Difficulty: Trails for all skill levels, beginner through advanced

Trail Length: 32 miles

Connects To: North Shore Mountains Ski Trail and Cascade River State Park

Maps: Map #5 of the North Shore Mountains Ski Trail, or state park brochure with map available from the Park Ranger.

Highlights: Largest deer yard in Minnesota, excellent variety of trails, beautiful Cascade River and falls, scenic vistas

Trailhead: Cascade Lodge and Cascade River State Park are the main trailheads for this system (see additional information about the park on page 59). The lodge is 7 miles northeast of Lutsen, adjacent to Highway 61. The State Park is ½ mile further northeast, also on the northwest side of the highway. Skiers need state ski licenses, and state park stickers are required for vehicles in the park.

Description: This splendid system of trails was one of the first to develop along the North Shore, and it is still one of the biggest and one of the best systems in the area. The interesting diversity of trails enables skiers to experience a wide variety of North Woods terrain — a cascading river, breathtaking panoramas from mountainous ridges, beaver ponds, an inland lake, and dense forests of cedar, spruce and hardwoods. Wildlife is abundant in this area. White-tailed deer congregate in the largest deer yard in Minnesota, and moose are common along parts of the trails. Where deer and moose are found, you can be sure that timber wolves are nearby, but sightings of these shy mammals are rare.

Long climbs up from the coast of Lake Superior enable good downhill runs for more experienced skiers in the vicinity of Cascade River, while the rolling upland region in the vicinity of Deeryard Lake is a delight for almost any skier.

Because of their location at higher elevations away from Lake Superior, the Deeryard lake trails are blanketed with good snow for a longer season than the trails situated closer to the big Lake. Don't be disheartened if you arrive in March for spring skiing to find slush and bare gound around Cascade Lodge. The upland trails may still be excellent.

The trails on the east side of the Cascade River are described in the section entitled Cascade River State Park (see page 59). They are connected to the trails on the west side of the river by a wooden bridge that spans a very scenic gorge. The partly frozen waterfalls present a fascinating scene, as viewed from the bridge high above. West of the river, a network of small loops parallel the Lake Superior shoreline in the vicinity of Cascade Lodge. Deer are frequently seen roaming right in the lodge's back yard.

Further inland, nearly six miles of intermediate trails loop up to the **Upper** and **Lower Ridge Runs** and to Lookout Mountain. The long climb from the lake is gradual, but rather exhausting for those not in good shape. But the long, downhill runs are delightful and make the effort well worthwhile. The **Lookout Mountain Trail** is double-tracked for two-way traffic. Near the summit, over 600 feet above Lake Superior, is a terrif view of Lake Superior and the bordering forests. A rest shelter is located there. Relax, build a fire and absorb the tranquilizing scene as you enjoy lunch in Nature's penthouse.

The **Deeryard Lake trails** extend even further inland, stretching northwest to Deeryard Lake. En route, the trail crosses a beaver pond in an area known to harbor moose. To the west of the pond, the trail climbs another 300 feet and then skirts the south side of an 1881-foot peak that towers over Deeryard Lake. For advanced skiers with energy to spare, a steep side trail leads one mile to the summit, where the old Cascade fire tower once stood.

Continuing west on the loop around the peak, skiers can fill their water bottles at a natural spring that flows out of a bank near the trail. Nearby is one of Minnesota's oldest yellow birch trees. The trail continues through lovely stands of spruce on a rolling landscape as it parallels the southeast shore of Deeryard Lake and beyond, to a point less than a mile from the Pike Lake Road (County Road 45).

The Babineau Corner on the Pike Lake Road is an alternate starting point for skiers who want to enjoy the Deeryard Lake trails, but without climbing more than a 1000 feet up from Lake Superior. In fact, one of the best way to enjoy these trails is to arrange shuttle service to the Babineau Corner, ski the Deeryard Lake loop, and then glide down the long runs to Cascade Lodge. It makes a splendid all-day outing.

FOR MORE INFORMATION: Contact Cascade Lodge, East Star Route 445, Lutsen, MN 55612. Or call (218) 387-1112.

Good Harbor Bay Loop

Use Level: Light

Trail Type: Machine groomed and track-set

Difficulty: Intermediate to Advanced

Trail Length: 2.2 miles

Connects To: North Shore Mountains Ski Trail

Maps: Map #5 of the North Shore Mountains Ski Trail, available from the Lutsen-Tofte Tourism Association

Trailhead: Thomsonite Beach Resort, located along Highway 61. 10 miles northeast of Lutsen.

Description: This trail begins at the bottom of Good Harbor Bay Rock Cut and follows the power line to the top of the "mountain," 400 feet above Lake Superior. It then passes through a birch forest and close to a rock cut, affording a breathtaking view of Lake Superior's rugged coastline.

From the west end of the loop, a connecting trail leads 2½ miles west, gradually climbing 300 feet to intersect the North Shore Mountains Trail corridor at a point ½ mile south of the Pike Lake Road. This trail is recommended for intermediate-level skiers.

FOR MORE INFORMATION: Contact Thomsonite Beach Resort, East Star Route Box 470, Lutsen, MN 55612. Or call (218) 387-1532.

Bally Creek Trails

Use Level: Light to Moderate

Trail Type: Machine groomed and track-set

Difficulty: Beginner to Intermediate

Trail Length: 5 miles

Connects To: North Shore Mountains Ski Trail

Maps: Map #5 of the North Shore Mountains Ski Trail, available from the Lutsen-Tofte Tourism Association

Highlights: High-country trails with good snowfall and long season.

Trailhead: 6 miles northwest of Grand Marais, along the Bally Creek Road (Forest Route #158)

Description: These two loops wind through gently rolling forested hills at an inland location that benefits from the heavy snowfall generated by Lake Superior, but far enough removed to escape the temperature-moderating effects of the lake that truncates skiing closer to the shore. Using groomed trails, beginners can enjoy the easy **Bally Creek Loop** (2.2 miles) and the southern part of the **Sundling Creek Loop.** But the hillier terrain crossed by the northern part of this loop is more suited to intermediate skiers.

This is the eastern end of the North Shore Mountains system of trails, and it's a good starting point for more experienced skiers who want to ski down to Lake Superior at Cascade River State Park, a beautiful ½-day route that covers almost 7 miles. Along the way, skiers will enjoy beautiful views of Lake Superior and the forested coastline.

FOR MORE INFORMATION: Contact Bear Track Outfitting Co., Box 51, Grand Marais, MN 55604. Or call (218) 387-1162.

NORTH SHORE MOUNTAINS LODGING

There is a splendid assortment of lodging accommodations along the North Shore of Lake Superior, ranging from moderately priced motels and rustic cabins, to deluxe lodges, condos and townhouses. Most have direct access to the ski trails of the North Shore Mountains system. A lodge-to-lodge program is available for skiers who would like to enjoy more than one lodging establishment. While guests ski from one lodge to another, their luggage is transferred for them. The participating resorts are located within a 25-mile stretch, along the length of the trail system. The maximum distance between neighboring resorts is only 5 to 6 miles, with some much closer. The following resorts are listed in geographical order, from southwest (closest to Duluth) to northeast (closest to Canada). For more information, contact the Lutsen-Tofte Tourism Association, Box 115, Lutsen, MN 55612, or any of the following resorts.

FENSTAD'S RESORT
OWNER/MANAGER: Blaine Fenstad
ADDRESS: 1190 Hwy 61 East, Little Marais, Silver Bay, MN 55614
PHONE: (218) 226-4724
LODGING: 7 modern housekeeping cabins accommodate 2-6 people.
AMENITIES: Fireplaces in all cabins; sauna planned.
COMMENTS: Fenstad's is a lovely resort on the beautiful shore of Lake Superior. It is 13 miles south of the North Shore Mountains Ski Trail system, but it maintains 16 km. of groomed ski touring trails on private property. The trail begins right at the resort, crosses Highway 61, and then follows a logging road to the highlands overlooking Lake Superior. Part of the trail system is suitable for beginners, while the ascent to Mountain Home Overlook (at 858 feet above the lake) is recommended for experts. Most of the trail system, however, is appropriate for intermediate skiers. Breathtaking overlooks highlight the area.

BLUEFIN BAY
OWNER/MANAGER: Mark Brown
ADDRESS: Tofte, MN 55615
PHONE: 1-800-862-3656
LODGING: Condominium apartments and townhouses.
COMMENTS: The Bluefin offers deluxe 1-3 bedroom accommodations with full kitchens, fireplaces and jaccuzzis overlooking Lake Superior, fine dining, cocktails and entertainment, as well as banquet and conference facilities. An access trail connects to the North Shore Mountains system.

CHATEAU LEVEAUX
MANAGER: Bill and Pauline Thomas
ADDRESS: Box 115, Tofte, MN 55615
PHONE: (218) 663-7223
LODGING: Complete housekeeping condominums, and motel units on and facing Lake Superior
AMENITIES: Indoor pool; whirlpool; sauna; game room; TV; in-room movies; fireplaces — all under one roof.
COMMENTS: Located about 6 miles southwest of the Lutsen Ski Area, Chateau Leveaux is focused on the family and couples who want a quiet, informal, yet modern facility. It is convenient to grocery, bottle shop, bank, lounges and restaurants. An access trail leads to the North Shore Mountains Trail.

COBBLESTONE CABINS
ADDRESS: Tofte, MN 55615
PHONE: (218) 663-7957
LODGING: Housekeeping cabins
AMENITIES: Wood-burning sauna
COMMENTS: Inexpensive rustic cabins with outdoor biffies overlook Lake Superior. Cross-country ski rentals and lessons (racing or touring) are available. There is direct access to the North Shore Mountains Ski Trail.

GULL HARBOR CONDOMINIUMS
MANAGER: Char Erickson
ADDRESS: Cliff Dweller Resort, U.S. Highway 61, Lutsen, MN 55612
PHONE: (218) 663-7273
LODGING: 6 Condominium suites and 2 deluxe cabins
AMENITIES: Sauna; whirlpool; fireplace; fully equipped for housekeeping
COMMENTS: Situated along the shore of Lake Superior, about midway between Tofte and Lutsen, Gull Harbor Condominiums provide luxurious accommodations for a minimum 2-night stay.

CLIFF DWELLER RESORT (Formerly Best Western Cliff Dweller)
OWNER/MANAGER: Char Erickson
ADDRESS: U.S. Highway 61, Lutsen, MN 55612
PHONE: (218) 663-7469
LODGING: Modern motel units with 2 double beds & private baths
DINING: Full-service restaurant open to the public 7 days a week.
AMENITIES: Color television; in-room movies; direct-dial telephones; gift shop; child care available by reservation; group meeting and party facilities
SPECIAL PROGRAMS: 3-day ski packages with Modified American Plan available, discounted for midweek visits.
COMMENTS: Best Western Cliff Dweller offers motel units that sit right on the shore of Lake Superior, with pleasant accommodations for one to four people. There is an access trail from the motel to the North Shore Mountains Ski Trail.

LUTSEN MOUNTAIN VILLAGE
MANAGER: Mark Crowl
ADDRESS: P.O. Box 26, Lutsen, MN 55612
PHONE: (218) 663-7241 or Toll Free 1-800-642-6036
LODGING: Ultra-modern housekeeping condominiums and townhouse apartments.
DINING: A restaurant and lounge with full menu is planned for the Village Square.
AMENITIES: Televisions and fireplaces in units, indoor pool and jacuzzi, child care center, ski lockers.
COMMENTS: The Village at Lutsen Mountains is an association of privately owned condominiums, townhouses and tourist-oriented businesses nestled in the beautiful Poplar River valley, adjacent to the Lutsen downhill Ski Area. Guests may ski directly from their doors to the network of Norpine trails that surrounds the Village or down an access trail that leads to the North Shore Mountains Trail. It is a lovely setting that is more typically associated with Colorado's downhill ski areas, such as Vail. The new condominium and townhouse units offer deluxe accommodations, the likes of which are not common in the Arrowhead region. Though still incomplete, plans call for the Village to include an assortment of shops for food, gifts, laundry, and a recreation center with sauna and ice skating area. Ski rentals are available.

The Village at Lutsen Mountains is an association of privately owned condos, townhouses and businesses overlooking the Lutsen alpine ski area.

Thoroughly modern accommodations are found at Lutsen Mountain Village.

Lutsen Resort offers completely modern accommodations in a quaint, Scandinavian atmosphere.

LUTSEN RESORT

OWNER/MANAGER: George Nelson, Jr.

ADDRESS: Lutsen, MN 55612

PHONE: (218) 663-7212 or Toll Free in Minnesota 1-800-232-0071 or Outside Minnesota 1-800-346-1467.

LODGING: Hotel rooms in Main Lodge with Modified American Plan, Cliff House with European Plan, or Sea Villa townhouses with completely furnished kitchens: Accommodations for 1-12 people.

DINING: Restaurant and cocktail lounge in Main Lodge.

AMENITIES: Indoor pool, saunas, whirlpool, game room, disco, conference rooms, phone and T.V. in motel rooms, fireplaces in townhouse apartments, all units have private shower baths.

SPECIAL PROGRAMS: Mid-week ski packages. Discounted rates for Spring Ski Special, midweek lodging, group packages, and Honeymooners: shuttle services offered.

COMMENTS: Lutsen Resort has long been one of the upper midwest's most attractive and popular resort facilities. Offering completely modern accommodations in a quaint, Scandinavian atmosphere, with direct access to the Lutsen Mountain Ski Area and the North Shore Mountains Ski Trail, this lovely resort also boasts a satisfying assortment of apres ski amenities that are found at few other lodges in the Arrowhead. Rates range considerably to reflect the wide choice of accommodations, from the economical Cliff House located near the Main Lodge, to the Sea Villa townhouses situated 2.8 miles south of the Main Lodge. All accommodations sit close to the shore of Lake Superior, and the view from the elegant dining room is superb. A Ski Touring Center, located along Highway 61 near the Lodge, provides ski rentals and sales of accessories. Shuttle service is available to cross-country trailheads at higher elevations in the Sawtooth Mountains.

CASCADE LODGE

OWNER/MANAGER: Gene and Laurene Glader
ADDRESS: H.C.R. 3, Box 445, Lutsen, MN 55612
PHONE: (218) 387-1112
LODGING: Rooms in the Main Lodge, motel and cabins provide accommodations for 2-8 people.
DINING: Full-service restaurant open to the public
AMENITIES: Game room, TV lounge with fireplace and piano, gift shop, babysitting services, cross-country equipment rentals, conference facilities.
SPECIAL PROGRAMS: Shuttle services available to skiing trailheads.
COMMENTS: Cascade Lodge and Restaurant rest along the scenic shore of Lake Superior, at the base of one of the oldest and best ski touring areas in the Arrowhead. Reasonable rates and a superb setting make this a popular destination for cross-country skiers in search of a challenging set of tracks. Its close proximity to Grand Marais allows easy access to a host of additional amenities, including a whirlpool and sauna at the municipal swimming pool. There is direct access from the Lodge to the North Shore Mountains Ski Trail.

Cascade Lodge sits at the base of one of the oldest and best ski touring areas in the Arrowhead.

SOLBAKKEN RESORT

OWNER/MANAGER: Beth and Bill Blank

ADDRESS: H.C.R. 3, Box 170, Lutsen, MN 55612

PHONE: (218) 663-7566

LODGING: Motel units with kitchenettes, 1-3 bedroom housekeeping cabins, and a 3 bedroom lakehome; accommodations for 1-8 people.

AMENITIES: Color T.V. in motel units; whirlpool-sauna complex, lounge, gift/book shop; also two new units designed to meet barrier-free standards for accessability by the handicapped.

SPECIAL PROGRAMS: Shuttle service available to ski trailheads.

COMMENTS: Solbakken Resort offers a variety of lodging accommodations in a rustic setting along the shore of Lake Superior, from the economical motel units to the deluxe lakehome. All overlook Lake Superior and include kitchen facilities. A 50-year-old lodge complex, formerly Sawbill Lodge, has been moved, log by log, from the shore of Sawbill Lake to Solbakken. It features a spectacular view of Lake Superior and a lounge area with a 10-foot-wide, floor-to-ceiling stone fireplace, as well as the whirlpool-sauna complex and an expanded gift/book shop. There is direct access to the Solbakken Ski Trails and the North Shore Mountains Ski Trail.

THOMSONITE BEACH

ADDRESS: E.S.R. Box 470, Lutsen, MN 55612

PHONE: (218) 387-1532

LODGING: Small and large luxury units, some with brick fireplaces and full kitchens.

AMENITIES: Satellite color TV

COMMENTS: Thomsonite Beach has direct access to the North Shore Mountains Trail and to the Good Harbor Bay Loop.

BEAR TRACK OUTFITTING COMPANY

OWNER/MANAGER: David and Cathi Williams

ADDRESS: Box 51, Grand Marais, MN 55604

PHONE: (218) 387-1162

LODGING: Rustic cabins accommodate up to 12 people, and Outpost Tent Cabins accessible only by ski or snowshoe.

SPECIAL PROGRAMS: Guided winter camping expeditions, accompanied by dog sleds, into Superior National Forest's interior and the BWCA Wilderness.

AMENITIES: Ski equipment rentals available; Finnish sauna

COMMENTS: Bear Track Outfitting Company's Bally Creek Camp is an inexpensive alternative for skiers who don't mind giving up modern amenities for a weekend, or longer. Wood-heated cabins have no electricity, no phones, no TV and, of course his and her outdoor privies. Guests provide their own sleeping bags, towels and cooking and eating utensils. Because of its inland location, at more than 900 feet above Lake Superior, snow conditions here are normally more dependable and longer lasting than at proximities closer to the lake.

At the Lake Superior end of the Grand Portage Trail is the re-creation of a 200-year-old North West Company trading post.

Grand Portage Area Trails

Use Level: Moderate

Trail Type: Machine groomed and track-set

Difficulty: Beginner through Advanced

Trail Length: 99 miles

Maps: Available at Grand Portage Lodge or the Tourist Information Center

Highlights: Outstanding panoramas; historic points of interest; a system of trails that are always well-groomed

Trailhead: Grand Portage is 145 miles northeast of Duluth, only five miles from the north end of Highway 61 at the Canadian border. Most of the trails begin at Trail Center located six miles northwest of Grand Portage Lodge on County Road 17.

Description: Grand Portage Reservation offers skiers one of the most extensive and best-groomed ski trail systems in the state. Scattered across the 56,000-acre reservation are sixteen different trails that allow for adequate disbursement of trail users, even on the busiest weekends. Under "normal" snow conditons, the only trail that is not groomed is the historic Grand Portage Trail, which is part of Grand Portage National Monument, administered by the National Park Service. The rest of the trails are double-tracked by a new Kassbohrer Pisten-Bully groomer that enables excellent trails even during poor snow conditions.

All of the trails are marked with red arrows, and the mileages on the trails are marked in one-mile intervals from beginning to end. For example, on a five-mile loop trail, the Trailhead is marked (5). The last mileage sign you encounter will be (1), indicating that you are one mile from the end. Directional signs route traffic throughout the system, and safety signs warn for caution at the tops of steep hills and sharp curves. A Trail Register is located in the lobby of Grand Portage Lodge, and users of the free trails are encouraged to sign out before skiing on the trails and then to sign in when finished. IF YOU SIGN OUT, BE SURE TO SIGN IN afterwards!

Grand Portage is steeped in history. At the Lake Superior end of the Grand Portage Trail is a re-creation of a 200-year-old North West Company trading post. Founded around 1778 and abandoned in 1803, this fort was the hub for North American commerce for 25 years. It is here that brigades of Voyageurs brought beaver pelts from northwestern Canada to rendezvous with traders from Montreal, who in turn transported the furs back to Montreal and eventually to European markets. The Grand Portage, or Great Carrying Place, was a burdensome 8½-mile overland journey from Lake Superior to the navigable waters of the Pigeon River at Fort Charlotte. Today, skiers and hikers can still travel over this historic route that was used for hundreds of years by the Indians and by the white explorers and Voyageurs who opened up the great Northwest to trade and eventually settlement.

The portage trail, which is part of Grand Portage National Monument, bisects the reservation of the Grand Portage Band of the Minnesota Chippewa Tribe. Aside from the Grand Portage Trail, itself, all of the other trails are on reservation property. There are no trail use fees.

The historic Grand Portage Trail is not groomed,
but it is usually skier tracked.

The **GRAND PORTAGE TRAIL** (9 miles one way): Managed by
the National Park Service, and not groomed for skiers, the Grand Portage
Trail begins at the reconstructed stockade and winds north and west to the
site of Old Fort Charlotte, 638 feet above Lake Superior. The first 3.6
miles of the trail climb steadily from the lake and then roll through a series
of hilltops and valleys, creating some fast and challenging ski runs. The upper end of the trail (4.9 miles) from Old U.S. Highway 61 to Fort Charlotte
on the Pigeon River is relatively flat, but far from dull. At one point, the
trail crosses a beaver pond on a well-designed boardwalk. Farther on,
stately virgin white pines grace the trailside. A short distance from Fort
Charlotte, a side trail cuts north to the Cascades, where the Pigeon River
plunges over 140 feet in less than ¼ mile through a rocky gorge. Spectacular scenery is to be found there. When nearing the gorge, use
EXTREME CAUTION. A rest cabin with wood stove and bunkbeds is
located nearby.

To ski the entire Grand Portage Trail to the Cascades and back takes an entire day, even for experienced skiers. It's too much for inexperienced skiers. The trail was designed for hikers, not for ski touring. Some downhill runs have sharp turns at the bottom, so use extra caution. For less experienced skiers, there are two good, abbreviated routes using the Grand Portage Trail. Intermediate skiers looking for a good downhill run may want to start at old Highway 61, 8 miles north of the present Highway 61 via County Road 17, and then ski back to the Grand Portage stockade. Beginners and intermediates alike will enjoy the route to the Cascades from old Highway 61. But even this shortened route is nearly 10 miles — a challenging distance for most beginners.

The **PARTRIDGE FALLS TRAIL** (10 miles round trip) follows an old roadway for five miles from old Highway 61 to the Pigeon River. Recommended for intermediate skiers, the trail crosses mostly rolling terrain, and there are a number of moderate downhill runs. The double-tracked trail passes a few large white pine trees and a beaver pond, following close to Partridge Creek, which is bordered on the south side by a high wooded ridge. The trail ends at a point on the Pigeon River about a quarter mile upstream from the falls, where the river cascades forty feet into a scenic, rocky gorge that extends a few hundred yards downstream. It is recommended that skiers remove their skis before approaching the falls area, where slippery ice and snow could be extremely treacherous. In midwinter, the frozen falls is a beautiful sight to behold.

The head of this popular trail is 5.8 miles from Highway 61, via County Road 17 through Mineral Center, three-quarter mile beyond Trail Center.

The Partridge Falls Trail ends at the Pigeon River, which forms the boundary between Canada and the U.S.

The **SUGAR BUSH TRAIL** (2.5-mile Loop) is a good route for beginners and more experienced skiers looking for a nice warm-up loop. It begins on the east side of County Road 17, near Trail Center, 5 miles west of Highway 61. The counter-clockwise loop is over nearly level terrain forested with sugar maple trees. A sharp turn toward the north in a large clearing marks the midpoint of this easy loop.

The **LOON LAKE TRAIL** (5-mile Loop) is an excellent route for intermediate skiers and plenty of challenge for most advanced skiers. Beginning at the Trail Center parking lot, five miles west of Highway 61, the trail begins with a long, gradual climb along a route shared with several other loops. Watch for signs to direct you around this clockwise loop that skirts the east end of Loon Lake. There are a couple of moderate downhill runs on the south and north sides of the loop, and a long, fast downhill run brings you back to the junction of the loop with the access trail from Trail Center. At the northeast corner of the loop is a panoramic view of the Partridge Creek Valley, from 1038 feet above Lake Superior. This trail passes through sugar maple forests where the Chippewa people have collected maple sap for centuries.

Like other trails in the Grand Portage Reservation, the Loon Lake Trail is groomed to perfection.

The **MOOSE RIDGE TRAIL** (10-mile Loop) is an intermediate loop that extends beyond the Loon Lake Trail. It combines the exciting downhill runs and the breathtaking views of the Loon Lake Trail with the wilderness solitude and more challenging distance of the Moose Ridge trail itself. Beginning at Trail Center and following the same access trail to and along the south side of the Loon Lake loop, this trail then continues west bound, past the south end of Loon Lake, where there is a scenic overlook. From that point on, the trail alternates between flat and gently rolling terrain. The forest habitat also alternates between the dense boreal forest of spruce, fir and cedar and the more open stands of climax hardwood sugar maple. A cedar swamp along the southern part of the loop is the winter home for moose. Sightings of this majestic mammal are possible for quiet skiers. An old logging shack is near the mid-point of the trail.

Trail Center marks the origin of most Grand Portage area trails.

The **MT. SOPHIE TRAIL** (7-mile Loop) begins at Trail Center and follows an intermediate route to the highest point on the Grand Portage Reservation. At 1,814 feet above sea level, the summit of Mt. Sophie towers 1,212 feet above Lake Superior and affords skiers an outstanding panorama of some of the most rugged landscape in the upper midwest. The trail first uses the same route as that of the Moose Ridge Trail to a junction just south of Loon Lake. From that point, the Mt. Sophie Trail veers toward the southwest, traversing small hills en route to the overlook spur trail. Near the peak is a rest cabin with a wood stove where skiers can catch their breath after the steep climb to the summit of Mt. Sophie. The downhill return trip seems even steeper. Less experienced skiers may prefer to walk, and advanced skiers should use caution. After rejoining the main loop from the spur trail to the cabin, there is another long, steep downhill run that bends to the right. This, too, requires caution. At its junction with the North Lake Trail, the Mt. Sophie Trail returns to the trailhead over rolling terrain with no hazards.

The steep trail down from the Mt. Sophie is often "groomed" by skiers.

93

Near the peak of Mt. Sophie is a rest cabin with a wood stove where skiers can catch their breath after the steep climb to the summit.

The North Lake Trail offers an easy route for intermediate skiers.

The **NORTH LAKE TRAIL** (11-mile Loop) is an extension from the south end of the Mt. Sophie loop. They join at a point just north of North Lake and just below the long, steep downhill curve on the Mt. Sophie Trail This 11-mile loop swings back toward the east and joins the southern parts of the 5 Dog and 3 Dog Loops to complete the round trip from Trail Center. For skiers with more ambition, a side-trip to Trout Lake will add four more miles to this intermediate route. A shorter detour to Taylor Lake adds just one additional mile to the loop. There are no steep downhill runs along the North Lake Trail, but there is a sharp switch-back curve just north of the Trout Lake spur trail. Approach it slowly.

North Lake Trail

The **SAWMILL TRAIL** (2.5-mile Loop) is the shortest of the loops originating at Trail Center. In a counter-clockwise direction, the trial begins with a gradual uphill climb along the main corridor access trail and then loops south to junctions with the 5 Dog and 3 Dog loops and then slopes back down to the trailhead. This is a quick warm-up loop for the distance skier, or a leisurely afternoon outing for the whole family. Beginners will have no problem negotiating the course.

The **5 DOG LOOP** (6 miles) extends from the southwest corner of the Sawmill Loop and shares a two-way trail with skiers returning from Mt. Sophie. It leads over pleasantly rolling terrain covered by forests of spruce, birch and sugar maple. At the south end of the loop, it joins the North Lake Loop and then heads northeast to the 3 Dog Loop, where skiers have the option of either returning north to Trail Center, or first circling northeast on the Section 11 Loop before ending their outings at Trail Center.

The **3-DOG LOOP** (4.2 miles) is one of the most beautiful ski trails on the Grand Portage Reservation, and one that beginners should have little trouble negotiating. For nearly three miles, the trail meanders through a young forest of pure white spruce, jack pine and Norway pine. An upturned labyrinth of weathered cedar roots marks the half way point of the trail.

The **SECTION 11 LOOP** (6.5 miles) heads east from the south end of the 3 Dog Loop, crosses County Road 17 at Mineral Center and continues in a counter-clockwise direction to the east end of the Sugar Bush Loop. The trail passes over gently rolling landscape and along several beaver ponds. Inexperienced skiers should have no problem with the loop. The trail follows the northern part of the Sugar Bush Loop back to Trail Center.

The **OLD HOMESTEAD TRAIL** (5 miles) is an extension of the 3-Dog Loop. Rated for intermediate skiers, the trail winds through the abandoned fields of two old homesteads that were settled in the early 1900's. After crossing a creek near the north end of the loop and passing the first homestead site, the trail begins a long uphill climb, en route to an open meadow where there is a scenic overlook of Lake Superior at 818 feet above the water. Afterwards there is a fast downhill run toward the second homestead site. Three more good downhill runs grace the remainder of the rolling trail, as it passes through fields that have been replanted with jack pine and Norway pine. The Old Homestead Trail may be combined with any one or more of the loops that connect with it: 3 Dog, 5 Dog or North Lake trails.

The **SKYLINE TRAIL** (9.3 miles) joins the network of trails emanating from Trail Center with the coastal trails near Grand Portage Lodge. It begins at the east end of the Sugar Bush Trail and then descends over 600 feet to Highway 61 and the Portage Valley Trail, just west of the lodge. Recommended for at least intermediate skiers, the first half of the trail passes over fairly easy, rolling terrain, but there are some fast downhill runs in the final 7 km of the route. A few sharp and difficult turns near the lake should challenge the most experienced skiers. Skiers should make prior arrangements to be shuttled back to their cars at Trail Center if they start from here. Or one can access the trails beginning at Trail Center directly from Grand Portage Lodge via the Portage Valley and Skyline trails.

The **PORTAGE VALLEY TRAIL** (4½-mile Loop) provides a short, challenging warm-up loop for skiers staying at Grand Portage Lodge. It can begin right at the back door of the lodge or across Highway 61 from the Information Center. With primarily flat to gently rolling terrain, the trail is rated for advanced beginning and intermediate skiers. For the more experienced skiers, there is access to a rock outcropping at the north end of the loop that affords a nice overlook of the surrounding valley. A short, fast. downhill run brings skiers back to the valley floor. Less experienced skiers may bypass this part of the trail.

A short **LIGHTED SKI TRAIL** (1¼ miles) begins at Grand Portage Lodge and loops across the flat terrain just south of the lodge. As the name suggests, the trail is lighted for skiers who haven't had enough skiing prior to sunset. This trail is easy enough for the most inexperienced beginners. Due to its close proximity to Lake Superior, however, the snow condition here is not likely to be as good as it is on the more elevated trails, especially early and late in the season.

FOR MORE INFORMATION about the whole network of Grand Portage ski trails, contact Grand Portage Lodge, P.O. Box 307, Grand Portage, MN 55605. For additional information about Grand Portage National Monument and the Grand Portage Trail, itself, contact The Superintendent, Grand Portage National Monument, P.O. Box 666, Grand Marais, MN 55604. Or call (218) 387-2788.

Grand Portage Lodge is an oasis of modern accommodations amidst a rustic environment of the primitive Northwoods landscape.

GRAND PORTAGE LODGE
OWNER/MANAGER: Grand Portage Band of Chippewa Indians
ADDRESS: Box 307, Grand Portage, MN 55605
PHONE: (218) 475-2401 or Toll Free in Minnesota: 1-800-232-1384
LODGING: 100 motel units
DINING: Full-service restaurant open to the public
AMENITIES: Indoor swimming pool, sauna, cocktail lounge with satellite television, lighted ski trail, Tourist Center, where one may rent skis or snowshoes, and buy snacks, souvenirs and gasoline.
SPECIAL PROGRAMS: Shuttle service to the Trail Center; resident ski touring expert available to assist skiers; Naturalist programs.
COMMENTS: Grand Portage Lodge is a paradox — a deluxe convention facility amidst the rugged northshore wilderness of the Grand Portage Indian Reservation; an oasis of modern accommodations amidst the rustic environment of primitive Northwoods forests.

With trails beginning at the door of the lodge, it is possible for guests to ski right into the elaborate system of superbly groomed trails.

Spacious motel rooms each contain two double beds, modern baths and television sets. Half the rooms overlook Lake Superior, while the other half views the scenic wooded slopes behind the lodge.

The Lodge dining room also overlooks the lake and features native Northwoods specialties, such as Lake Superior trout, caught locally, wild rice, and homemade cornbread and pastries.

The large swimming pool and sauna are open 24 hours a day, and they offer great places to relax after a strenuous day of cross-country skiing.

The conference center provides an extraordinary setting for meetings, conferences, seminars, workshops and banquets. 3,600 square feet of space will accommodate up to 300 people.

97

Skiers cross Gunflint Lake en route to the East End Trail.

CHAPTER 5

THE GUNFLINT TRAIL

The Gunflint Trail — Cook County Road #16 — is a delightfully winding, hilly and scenic highway that connects the North Shore community of Grand Marais with the Boundary Waters Wilderness. From many points along its 58-mile course, cross country skiers may penetrate the federal wilderness on the frozen lakes and streams and snow-covered portage trails that have been used by canoeists for hundreds of years.

For skiers who prefer nicely groomed trails in a rustic wilderness setting, the Gunflint Trail area offers nearly 100 miles of ski trails, most in a continuous network stretching from East Bearskin Lake northwest to the Canadian border at Gunflint Lake. The densely forested landscape is typically rolling, but is accentuated by steep ridges that afford panoramic overlooks. Intermediate-level skiers should find the entire system appealing. There are also some good trails for beginners and plenty of challenge for the experts.

Grand Marais is the commercial center for the Gunflint Trail. There, winter visitors will find motels and hotels, restaurants, laundry facilities and a terrific municipal indoor swimming pool with sauna that is available to tourists. Along the Gunflint Trail, itself, are several fine resorts that offer skiers an interesting and varied assortment of lodging accommodations that blend quite nicely into the peaceful wilderness setting. For more information write the Tip of the Arrowhead Association, Grand Marais, MN 55604.

A nice municipal swimming pool and sauna are available to tourists in Grand Marais.

The Gunflint Trail connects the North Shore community of Grand Marais with the Boundary Waters Wilderness.

Pincushion Mountain Ski Trail

Use Level: Moderate

Trail Type: Machine groomed and track-set

Difficulty: Trails for all skiing abilities — Mostly Intermediate and Advanced.

Trail Length: 11.1 miles

Maps: Available from the Tourist Information Center in Grand Marais

Highlights: Good variety of trails; panorama at Pincushion Mountain

Trailhead: At the Sawtooth Mountain Scenic Overlook, ¼ mile southeast of County Road 12 (Gunflint Trail), 2 miles north of Grand Marais.

Description: Located only a couple miles from, yet several hundred feet higher than, Grand Marais, this scenic system of trails is one of the best in the area. Offering a variety of trail lengths and difficulties, there is something for everyone — beginner through expert skiers. The trails wind through a lovely hardwood forest that affords nice views of river valleys and distant ridges. Single and double-tracked trails are usually groomed once a week by the local Ski and Run Club, and all intersections are clearly marked with "You are here" maps.

The trail starts at a large parking lot at the scenic overlook and climbs a short slope, before descending to the first intersection where the beginner, intermediate and advanced loops begin. Beginners wind counter-clockwise through a 1½-mile loop just north of the parking lot. Intermediates continue skiing east to a 3.75-mile intermediate loop that passes over several small hills en route to the best scenery in the system. After 1¼ miles, the trail reaches a ridge that parallels 200 feet above the Devils Track River. This marks the beginning of the "Rim Run," which gives skiers almost a mile of gentle downhill gliding and impressive views of Devils Track Canyon before reaching Pincushion Mountain. To climb to the summit, skiers must remove their skis and walk to the spectacular overlook, 558 feet above Lake Superior. After a caution hill at the southeast end of the loop, the trail levels out for about a mile and then gradually climbs back to the trailhead.

A network of advanced trails weaves throughout the hilly northwestern part of the ski area. There, the more ambitious skiers will find a mixture of steep hills and sharp corners that all add up to about 4 miles of skiing pleasure. Most of the loops are one-way. They may be combined with other loops for a longer or more varied skiing experience.

A 1¼-mile connecting trail leads downhill from the parking area to the high school in Grand Marais. Student skiers frequently use the trail system. Another short spur at the northwest corner of the system connects to the Pincushion Mountain Cross Country Center, where rentals, waxes and hot drinks are available for skiers.

FOR MORE INFORMATION: Contact Gunflint Ranger District, United States Forest Service, Grand Marais, MN 55604. Or call (218) 387-1750 for current snow conditions.

George Washington Memorial Pine Plantation Trail

Use Level: Light

Trail Type: Natural environment trail, not groomed, but usually skier-tracked.

Difficulty: Beginner

Trail Length: 1½ miles (Round trip)

Maps: Available from the Tourist Information Center in Grand Marais

Highlights: Easy trail for beginning skiers; pine plantation

Trailhead: On the left (west) side of the Gunflint Trail (County Road 12), six miles north of Highway 61 in Grand Marais.

Description: Although this trail is neither groomed nor marked, it is frequently used, almost always has tracks on it, and it is easy to follow. The trail runs through the George Washington Memorial Pine Plantation, a 32-acre plot where Norway and white pines were planted in 1932, five years after a fire destroyed much of the forest in this area. The trail continues in a northwest direction over nearly level terrain and ends on the east edge of Elbow Creek, ¾ miles from the parking lot.

FOR MORE INFORMATION: Contact the Gunflint Ranger District, United States Forest Service, Grand Marais, MN 55604. Or call (218) 387-1750 for current snow conditions.

GRAND MARAIS AREA LODGING

Grand Marais is a bustling little town that serves skiers in this part of the Arrowhead. Accommodations there include motels, restaurants, supermarkets, service stations, a laundromat and a variety of other stores. Recreational facilities in Grand Marais include a skating and hockey rink, a curling club, a bowling alley and a municipal swimming pool, with whirlpool and sauna. An airport is located northeast of town, and a bus line provides daily service to the community.

Several motels and lodges are located in or near Grand Marais:

EAST BAY HOTEL:
OWNER: James and Lois Pedersen
ADDRESS: Grand Marais, MN 55604
PHONE: (218) 387-2800
ACCOMMODATIONS: Hotel rooms sleep one to four, private bath, cable TV, telephone.
DINING: Dining Room features old fashioned "from scratch soups and specials and home-baked Swedish rye bread.
COMMENTS: Built in 1906, East Bay Hotel is an historic Inn located in downtown Grand Marais, on the beach of Lake Superior. The dining room and many of the guest rooms overlook Lake Superior.

The **TIP OF THE ARROWHEAD ASSOCIATION** lists the following additional motels and lodges that are available for winter guests:

LUND'S COTTAGE COURT & MOTEL: Box 126, Grand Marais, MN 55604

SKYPORT LODGE: SR3 Box 478, Grand Marais, MN 55604

WINDIGO LODGE: Box 67, Gunflint Trail, Grand Marais, MN 55604

SHORELINE MOTOR LODGE: Grand Marais, MN 55604

SANDGREN MOTEL: Box 355, Grand Marais, MN 55604

TOMTEBODA MOTEL: Grand Marais, MN 55604

GUNFLINT MOTEL: Grand Marais, MN 55604

LIND'S MOTOR COURT: Grand Marais, MN 55604

SUPERIOR INN — BEST WESTERN: Box 456-T, Grand Marais, MN 55604

NOR'WESTER LODGE: Box 60TA, Grand Marais, MN 55604

ASPENWOOD MOTEL: Box 130L, Tofte, MN 55615

Central Gunflint Ski Trails

Use Level: Moderate

Trail Type: Machine groomed and track-set

Difficulty: Mostly intermediate, some beginner and advanced

Trail Length: 25½ miles

Maps: Available at Golden Eagle or Bearskin Lodges

Fee: For maps and parking; no trail use fees.

Highlights: Very nicely groomed trail through a variety of terrain: Scenic overlooks.

Connects to: Banadad Artery Trail

Trailhead: This trail system is anchored by Bearskin Lodge on the south and Golden Eagle Lodge on the north. Golden Eagle Lodge is located on the north shore of Flour Lake, 2½ miles northeast of the Gunflint Trail via the Clearwater Road, 27 miles north of Grand Marais. Bearskin Lodge is on the northwest shore of East Bearskin Lake, about a mile northeast of the Gunflint Trail, 26 miles north of Grand Marais.

Description: Few trail systems — anywhere — can boast such a splendid network of expertly groomed and tracked ski trails. The trails sit on the very edge of the Boundary Waters Canoe Area Wilderness and wind through a varied landscape of rolling hills covered with spruce and aspen, spruce bogs, spectacular cliffs, stands of virgin pine and frozen lakes. Most of the trails are ideally suited to intermediate skiers — trails that require a fair amount of proficiency to negotiate the rolling terrain — but there is plenty of good skiing for beginners and some challenging parts of the system for advanced skiers. All parts of the system can be reached from either lodge in a comfortable day's outing. Though most of the trails are in the vicinity of East Bearskin and Flour lakes, one of the nicest loops extends across the Gunflint Trail into a lovely, rolling region where skiers have the best chance of seeing big game. The trails are double-tracked and clearly marked with directional signs.

Although these trails receive more use than many trails in the Arrowhead, there are plenty of loops designed to disburse people. The result is a feeling of light use across the network of trails, in spite of other skiers present on weekends.

Because so much attention has been paid to good trail surfaces, a Kassbohrer Pisten-Bully groomer enables excellent ski trails even during poor snow conditions. More surfacing improvements are planned for the future, which will ensure that these trails will continue to be some of the best in the entire state.

The **OX CART TRAIL** (3.2 miles) begins at Bearskin Lodge and leads west, across the East Bearskin Road, to a lowland area characterized by beaver ponds and aspen swamps. The trail then climbs over 50 feet and bends back toward the east to follow a highland ridge cloaked with pine. This a good warm-up loop for intermediate skiers, and it's a nice half-day outing in itself for beginners.

The double-tracked Ox Cart Trail follows a delightful route that was used in the early 1900's.

The **POPLAR CREEK TRAIL** (6.3 miles) branches off the Ox Cart Trail just after it crosses the East Bearskin Lake Road. The trail first leads to a large gravel pit, where more experienced skiers may want to practice their downhill techniques. Novice skiers, on the other hand, may be inclined to remove their skis and walk up the steep slope. Above (south of) the pit, the trail parallels the Gunflint Trail for a short distance and then crosses the road. .7 Km further, the trail splits into a loop. Following the loop in a clockwise direction, skiers gradually descend to pass between Quiver and Bow lakes. After crossing an old summer road, skiers can enjoy a delightful combination of rolling small hills, lowland bog and creekside marsh. The north side of the loop passes through a dense stand of young spruce on rolling hills and returns skiers to the loop's junction in an old logging area. Starting at Bearskin Lodge, the entire route is 7½ miles — a great afternoon outing for intermediate skiers, or a challenging all-day trek for those with less experience.

The **BEAVER DAM TRAIL** (5.6 miles round trip from Bearskin Lodge) begins at Bearskin Lodge and leads northeast for 1.7 Km as it parallels the south side of the Summer Home Road (an extension of the East Bearskin Lake Road). After crossing to the north side of the road, the trail splits and forms a 3½-mile loop around Ruby and Rudy lakes. Hilly terrain creates some swift downhill runs, as well as several outstanding panoramas. A rest shelter sits on a high ridge above the south shore of Flour Lake. At the west end of Ruby Lake are the results of beaver activity. Although parts of this trail are easy enough for novice skiers, most of the route is better suited to intermediate-level skiers. There is plenty of challenge for advanced skiers, too.

The **OLD LOGGING CAMP TRAIL** (6.6 miles) intersects the Beaver Dam Trail at the west end of Rudy Lake and the east end of Ruby Lake. When combined with the northern part of the Beaver Dam Trail, the Old Logging Camp Trail circles Flour Lake. From Golden Eagle Lodge, the total distance is just over 8.1 miles. Using the southern part of the Beaver Dam Trail and all of the Old Logging Camp Trail, the distance from Bearskin Lodge is almost 11 miles. Although the northern part of the loop incorporates some old logging railroad beds, which are relatively level, the entire loop is probably too much for novice skiers. And the western end and bottom parts of the loop have some challenging hills. Along the route are several scenic viewpoints, and an impressive stand of virgin white pine and a glacial ridge between Wampus and Flour lakes are further highlights of this long loop.

The Old Logging Camp Trail can be extended on the north side of the loop by detours of 1½ miles on the Red Pine Trail and ¼ mile on the Moose Ridge Trail. The **RED PINE TRAIL** begins on an old railroad grade and then winds and climbs through a pine forest to a ridge with fine views of West Bearskin Lake to the west and Clearwater Lake to the northeast. Further east on the ridge, the trail crosses a clearing where skiers may view south across Flour Lake. The trail then drops rather quickly back down to the Old Logging Camp Trail. Beginners should probably avoid this detour, which descends nearly 200 feet in less than half a mile.

The **MOOSE RIDGE TRAIL** is even more difficult, and it is recommended for only advanced skiers. It abruptly climbs from the north shore of Flour Lake to the summit of a hill that rises nearly 140 feet above the lake. The panoramic view across Flour Lake and north towards the Canadian border is breathtaking.

Less experienced skiers can bypass the hilly southern part of the Beaver Dam Trail by skiing on the **SUMMER HOME ROAD,** a 1¼-mile stretch over gently rolling hills that connects the east end of the Old Logging Camp Trail with Bearskin Lodge, via a 1-mile stretch of the Beaver Dam Trail.

FOR MORE INFORMATION: Contact either Bearskin Lodge, Box 10W Gunflint Trail, Grand Marais, MN 55604 or Golden Eagle Lodge, Box GT 27B, Grand Marais, MN 55604.

Some of the best groomed trails in Minnesota are found in the Central Gunflint area.

Bearskin Lodge and Ski Touring Center offers amenities that are found at few other winter resorts in the Arrowhead . . .

. . . including an 8-person hot tub Jacuzzi bath.

LODGING

There are two lodges adjacent to the Central Gunflint Trails system, Bearskin Lodge on East Bearskin Lake and Golden Eagle Lodge on Flour Lake. Both provide trail maps for their guests.

BEARSKIN LODGE SKI TOURING CENTER

OWNER/MANAGER: Barb & Dave Tuttle

ADDRESS;   Gunflint Trail Box 10G, Grand Marais, MN 55604

PHONE: (218) 388-2292 or Toll Free Outstate: 1-800-328-3325 Instate: 1-800-622-3583

LODGING: 4 housekeeping cabins; 4 2-story apartments adjacent to the lodge: Maximum accommodation level: 58 people

DINING: Family-style meals served in the main lodge, by reservation.

AMENITIES: Cozy fireside ski lounge, gift shop with waxes and accessories, ski equipment rentals, X-C Ski School, guided ski tours, private sauna, 8-person hot tub Jacuzzi bath, waxing and ski storage room, kerosene lighted 2.5 km ski trail.

SPECIAL PROGRAMS: Lodge-to-lodge ski trips available; night ski tours with head lamps; Guided tours into the Boundary Waters Canoe Area Wilderness; Mid-week discounts on lodging (except Holidays).

COMMENTS: Bearskin Lodge Ski Touring Center probably hosts more cross-country skiers than any other resort in the Arrowhead. Catering only to skiers and snowshoers, this beautiful, modern resort entertains about 1500 skiers each winter. Sitting at the edge of the Boundary Waters Wilderness, the rustic setting paradoxically contains amenities that are found at few other winter resorts in northeastern Minnesota and front-door access to more than 35 miles of ski trails. In spite of all the skiers who enjoy staying here, guests do not feel crowded on the extensive trail system.

Secluded housekeeping cabins have two or three bedrooms that afford privacy for families or small groups. The two-story apartments next to the lodge can each accommodate up to 8 people and, combined, they are ideal for large family groups and ski clubs. Most units have fireplaces or wood-burning stoves. Pets are not allowed.

GOLDEN EAGLE LODGE

OWNER/MANAGER: John and Irene Baumann

ADDRESS: Gunflint Trail Box 27, Grand Marais, MN 55604

PHONE: (218) 388-2203 or Toll Free for reservations only 1-800-247-0591

LODGING: 2 & 3 bedroom housekeeping cabins

DINING: Evening meals are available by reservation only.

AMENITIES: Sauna; outside electrical receptacles for engine heaters.

SPECIAL PROGRAMS: Midweek discounts on lodging (except holidays).

COMMENTS: Golden Eagle Lodge offers a quiet family atmosphere and has secluded lakeshore cabins that are modern and completely furnished for housekeeping. Each unit will accommodate 6-8 people. The cabins have fireplace stoves and gas wall heaters. Groomed and tracked trails start right at the cabin doors.

The Banadad Artery Trail

Use Level: Light

Trail Type: Machine groomed and usually track-set

Difficulty: Intermediate level primarily

Trail Length: 16.2 miles

Maps: Available at Young's Homestead, and at other "Ski Through" lodges

Fee: For maps and parking at resorts along the Gunflint Trail

Highlights: Primitive route through the BWCAW; good area for moose

Connects to: Central Gunflint Ski Trails and Gunflint Lake Area Trails

Trailhead: The Banadad Artery Trail is a link between the Central Gunflint Ski Trails and the Gunflint Lake Area Trails. It is accessible from either end, as well as from Young's Homestead on Poplar Lake.

Description: The Banadad Artery Trail is a groomed wilderness trail that connects the Gunflint Lake area with the East Bearskin Lake area trails. Much of it is within the Boundary Waters Canoe Area Wilderness, where the trail is not always track-set, but usually it is single-tracked. Skiers are able to capture a sense of true backcountry solitude, as the trail leads to numerous unbroken wilderness trails that loop into the BWCAW. This affords a unique and contrasting experience from that in the Central Gunflint area, where the trails are groomed and track-set to perfection. Some skiers might find this experience more challenging and rewarding, while others prefer the emotional and physical security of the ridged tracks that are found at either end of the Gunflint system of trails.

The Banadad Trail is designed for lodge-to-lodge "ski-through" guests. There are no short loops leading to access roads where skiers may shuttle cars for half-day outings. On the contrary, the only plowed road that is crossed is the Gunflint Trail — once near East Bearskin Lake, and again near the west end of Loon Lake, almost 18 miles further down the Banadad Trail. Only expert skiers would attempt the whole route in one day. Most skiers break up the trail into two or three segments, spending nights at either Young's Homestead or the E.J. Croft Memorial Hut, or both. (See Lodge to Lodge Skiing Program for more details, page 111.)

Traveling from east to west, the Banadad Artery Trail begins at the northwest corner of the Poplar Creek Loop, 2.9 miles southwest of Bearskin Lodge. From there, it enters the Boundary Waters Wilderness, where it follows the path of an old logging road part of the way through the wilderness. 2.4 miles west of the Poplar Creek Loop is a spur trail leading north to Young's Homestead on Poplar Lake. About a mile further on the trail is the junction of the Gaskin Lake Wilderness Trail, which leads south to Caribou and Horseshoe lakes and on to Gaskin Lake. Continuing westbound, skiers pass an old Kimberly-Clarke logging camp about three miles west of the Gaskin Trail junction.

A fairly steep hill is encountered where the trail veers north to cross Banadad Creek. A short distance beyond that point is the junction of a trail leading north to the E.J. Croft Memorial Hut, which sits just outside the BWCA Wilderness, one mile from the Banadad Artery Trail. From the junction of the spur trail to the Gunflint Trail is 6½ miles. At that point, the Banadad joins up with the Gunflint Lake area trails.

Throughout its course, the Banadad Artery Trail passes over terrain that alternates from densely wooded landscape to lowland marshes and spruce bogs. Moose frequent the area, and sightings by quiet skiers are not uncommon. 'A lucky skier might also view a timber wolf. Where moose winter, wolves are sure to be nearby. In fact, a moose kill was once reported along the trail, just south of Banadad Creek.

FOR MORE INFORMATION: Contact the Gunflint Ranger District, United States Forest Service, Grand Marais, MN 55604, or any of the resorts that participate in the Gunflint Ski-Through Program.

Young's Asian Mongolian yurt is one of the most unique lodging accommodations in the Arrowhead region.

Inside the E.J. Croft Memorial Hut, a Mongolian "house tent."

LODGING

The only lodging facilities along the Banadad Trail that cater to cross-country skiers belong to Boundary Country Trekking, one of the most unique "resorts" in the Arrowhead.

BOUNDARY COUNTRY TREKKING

OWNER/MANAGER: Barbara and Ted Young, Steve McCrady

ADDRESS: Gunflint Trail 67-1, Grand Marais, MN 55604

PHONE: (218) 388-4487

LODGING: Youngs' Island Bed and Breakfast (limit of 4), Meeds Lake Hut and E.J. Croft Midtrail Hut (limit of 6 each)

DINING: An assortment of meal plans available, including their specialties, fruit stuffed Cornish hens with wild rice and Mongolian Fire Pot cuisine

AMENITIES: Sauna

SPECIAL PROGRAMS: Hut to hut skiing; day and overnight backcountry dog sled supported camping trips into the BWCA; participant in the Gunflint Trail lodge-to-lodge ski adventure

COMMENTS: Boundary Country Trekking is truly a unique enterprise. To call it a "resort" is misleading, to say the least. There is no lodge in the traditional sense.The Young family opens their house to guests and operate a hut to hut ski system along the 25 mile Banadad trail. On the island you stay in the guestroom of the Youngs fifty-year-old log home. Their house is a Minnesota Historic Bed and Breakfast home. Meals are served at the family table. A tracked trail from the island connects to the Banadad trail. On the trail are the most unique accommodations of all, the huts. The huts are an adaptation of a Mongolian yurt, a round structure traditionally used by Asiatic nomads. The huts are fully equipped for overnight stays with cots, cooking facilities and wood heat. Boundary Country Trekking provides the food and acts as hut hosts, or guests may bring and cook their own food. Either way, Boundary Country Trekking transports food and gear. The huts are ten miles apart enabling guests to ski the BWCA, while spending the nights in comfortable, warm surroundings. Boundary Country Trekking offers a variety of ski treks or one can create his or her own. For example, The Gourmet Hut Trek includes dinner and accommodations on the island, ten miles of skiing, Mongolian Fire Pot dinner at a hut and a dog sled trip. On the Banadad Hut to Hut Challenge, guests ski the entire Banadad trail spending the nights at Youngs' Island and the two huts. Rates vary from one program to another. Flexibility seems to be the motto at Boundary Country Trekking.

Dog sled trips add new dimensions to Arrowhead vacations along the Gunflint Trail. (Photo courtesy of Ted Young, Boundary Country Trekking)

LODGE-TO-LODGE SKIING PROGRAM

Four resorts along the Gunflint Trail have formed the Gunflint Trail Lodge-to-Lodge Ski-Through Association: Bearskin Lodge at the east end of the Banadad Trail, Borderland and Gunflint lodges at the west end, and Young's Island Guest Room and wilderness huts near the center. Skiers start at one lodge and ski to one or more other lodges. These resorts are spaced appropriately to allow comfortably day outings. Your luggage and car are moved on ahead, to be waiting for you at the next lodge. Several package plans are available, from three to 5 nights, with varying rates. Custom trips may also be arranged. The program includes all meals, accommodations, saunas, maps and gear and car transfers. All a skier must carry is a day pack with trail munchies and a small amount of gear and clothing for emergencies. Cross-country skiing may be combined with dog sled trips. The Banadad Trail, combined with the Central Gunflint Trails and the Gunflint Lake Area Trails, offers skiers nearly 100 miles of trails to explore. There are shelters and huts scattered throughout the system. Skiing lodge to lodge is, by far, the best way to experience the widest variety of ski trails and an excellent assortment of resort facilities.

For more details, or to place reservations, contact any of the participating resorts, or call the central toll-free number: Instate 1-800-328-3362 / Outstate 1-800-328-3325.

The Highlands Trail affords some excellent views of Gunflint Lake through stands of birch and aspen.

Gunflint Lake Area Trails

Use Level: Light to Moderate

Trail Type: Machine groomed and track-set

Difficulty: Trails for all skill levels, beginner to advanced.

Trail Length: 41.5 miles

Maps: Available at Borderland Lodge, Gunflint Lodge, or Heston's Country Store and Cabins

Highlights: Nice variety of groomed trails in a wilderness setting; Scenic overlooks

Connects to: Banadad Artery Trail

Trailhead: These trails are along both sides of the Gunflint Trail, 42 miles northwest of Grand Marais, anchored by Borderland Lodge on the northwest corner of Gunflint Lake, and Gunflint Lodge and Heston's Country Store and Cabins on the south shore of the lake.

Description: This is a lovely system of superb trails that offers skiers the best of all worlds: good tracks on miles of well-groomed trails that disburse skiers in all directions, to virtually eliminate the likelihood of encountering "crowds"; a sense of experiencing the wilderness in a way that usually requires "breaking trail"; incredible panoramas and good possibilities of seeing Nature's epitome of Northwoods wildness: the majestic moose.

All of the trails are groomed and set with an excellent track, using equipment that was used at the Lake Placid Olympics. The trail developers made an effort to keep their trails narrow — wide enough for only a single set of tracks — to permit skiers to blend with the environment. In addition, because of its remote location, the network of trails is used primarily by the guests of the three lodges located there. Even on the busiest of holiday weekends, the trail system is large enough to absorb the influx of skiers, without sacrificing anyone's privacy or desire for wilderness solitude.

There is a good assortment of trails for all types of skiers, beginner to expert. Summer roads and old railroad beds are used for the easiest routes through some lovely terrain that even a first-time skier can enjoy. At the other end of the spectrum, experts will find challenging hills in the rugged landscape bordering the southwest side of the lake. Most of the trails, though, are ideal for intermediate skiers, offering a pleasant variety of rolling hills with occasional downhill runs and short climbs, mixed with nearly level stretches along wooded ridges that afford breathtaking vistas of Gunflint Lake and the Canadian wilderness beyond. Three-sided warming huts are scattered over the area for lunch or rest stops.

After completing the series of loops around Gunflint Lake, the long-distance skier may also join up with the west end of the Banadad Artery Trail and ski through an even lighter used region where moose yard during the winter, south of the Gunflint Trail.

A warming shelter sits near the east end of the Magnetic Rock Trail.

The **BIG PINE LOOP** (2 miles) begins and ends right behind Gunflint Lodge. Recommended for intermediate skiers, it loops up along the densely wooded hillside to an overlook that affords a nice view of Gunflint Lake. There is one longer hill, in particular, that might cause problems for inexperienced skiers.

The **OVERLOOK TRAIL** (.6 mile) begins at the west corner of the Big Pine loop. It is a fairly easy connecting trail that joins up with the West End and Highland trails. It is relatively level along much of it course, but climbs gently to its junction with County Road 12, where there is a short, but steep climb to the road.

The **HIGHLANDS TRAIL** (2.5 miles) is a beautiful route that continues where the Overlook Trail left off. After crossing County Road 12, skiers will climb very gradually along a north-facing slope of hardwoods that affords some excellent views of Gunflint Lake and the Canadian wilderness. (Don't forget to look over your right shoulder during the climb, or you might miss the scene!) After passing the first junction with the Ham Lake Trail, the Highlands Trail crosses several small hills en route to the grand climax near the end. As the trail bends toward the north, skiers encounter one of the biggest and fastest downhill runs in the area, affectionately called "wipe out hill." The trail follows an elongated "S" pattern, bending first to the left and then to the right, as it rapidly descends to the Cross River valley below. Most of the trail could be negotiated by intermediate-level; but inexperienced skiers should use a good deal of caution at "wipe out hill." If you prefer to walk, do so off to the side of the trail.

113

"Wipe out hill" is a challenge to even the most experienced of skiers.

The **HAM LAKE TRAIL** (3 miles) loops off of the Highland Trail. It leads south into an open area of new growth where moose are known to yard in the winter. Quiet skiers will have a good opportunity to see these awesome creatures. The wide-open landscape permits greater visibility of the countryside. But it also offers little protection from frigid northwest winds. Be prepared for arctic blasts while crossing this barren region. A warming shelter sits at the southwest corner of the loop. Skiers with only limited experience should have little difficulty skiing this trail, which crosses gently rolling terrain.

The **ASPEN ALLEY TRAIL** (1 mile) intersects the Highlands Trail near the base of "wipe out hill." It's an easy trail that leads east and parallels close to County Road 12, then intersects the road, and then continues on toward the north and east to intersect the River and Power Line trails.

The **RIVER TRAIL** (1 mile) intersects the Aspen Alley Trail on the east and County Road 12 on the west. In between, it passes over and around some small hills in the region just east of the Cross River. This short trail is recommended for intermediate skiers.

Magnetic rock attracts skiers, as well as compass needles.

The **POWER LINE TRAIL** (2 miles) leads north from the east end of the Aspen Alley and River trails to the west end of Gunflint Lake at Borderland Lodge. It's generally an easy trail, but there are some small hills that might challenge a beginner. The trail follows the open powerline cut that parallels the access road to Borderland Lodge, twice intersecting the West End Trail.

The **WARRENS ROAD TRAIL** (2.5 miles) follows an old summer road along the north side of the Cross River that terminates on the northwest corner of Gunflint Lake. It's an easy trail over nearly level terrain that connects the west end of the Highlands Trail with the Magnetic Rock Trail and the Cut Across Trail. Even the most inexperienced beginning skiers should have no difficulty on this pleasing route.

The **MAGNETIC ROCK TRAIL** (4 miles) passes through a scenic region of rolling hills, dense forests, open meadows and a small pond. Near the middle of the trail is the 60' high "Magnetic Rock" — large glacial debris left by glaciers 10,000 years ago. Recommended for intermediate skiers, this trail has some swift downhill runs and fairly steep uphill climbs that might be too difficult for most beginners. The trail intersects the Warrens Road Trail at its east end and County Road 12 on the west end. Open vistas near the west end afford skiers some nice views of the surrounding countryside. Near the east end is a warming shelter.

A man-made "canyon" lines parts of the East End Trail, along the north shore of Gunflint Lake.

A warming shelter is a popular rest stop for skiers using the Ham Lake Trail.

The **EAST END TRAIL** (5 miles one-way) uses an old railroad bed to parallel the Canadian shore of Gunflint Lake. It begins near "Charlie's cabin", just east of the outlet from Gunflint Lake into Magnetic Lake. The treetop canopy over the trail gives skiers the impression of a veritable winter wonderland. The trail also passes through narrow "canyons" that were created with the construction of the railroad. A cross carved in one of the rock ledges marks the spot where a railroad construction worker lost his life. Near the middle of the trail is a warming shelter where skiers may rest and enjoy their trail snacks. The nearly level terrain along the north shore of Gunflint Lake is ideally suited for beginning skiers. The trail is nicely groomed and single-tracked from Magnetic Lake to the warming shelter, and then across Gunflint Lake to Heston's resort. But the east end of the trail may not be groomed and tracked.

A cross carved in a rock ledge marks the spot where a railroad construction worker died — now bordering the East End Trail.

The **WEST END TRAIL** (4 miles) connects the Borderland Lodge area with the west end of Loon Lake, intersecting a number of trails en route. It crosses rather hilly terrain that can be fast in spots. The trail is recommended for intermediate and advanced skiers — "the better skiers who enjoy a challenge." It intersects the Powerline Trail, the Overlook Trail and the South Rim Trail, and ends at the Loon Lake landing.

The **SOUTH RIM TRAIL** (4 miles) intersects the West End Trail in the rugged highlands directly south of Gunflint Lodge. Steep climbing is required to reach the trail, but the reward is well worth the effort. The trail follows a very high ridge paralleling the south shore of Gunflint Lake, where skiers are treated to many excellent panoramas across Gunflint Lake and the distant Canadian hills. What goes up must come down. So it's only natural to expect a big downhill run from the scenic ridge back to the road, or further down to the lake at Heston's Country Store and Cabins. All in all, the trail is recommended for more experienced skiers who like a good challenge.

A spectacular panorama is enjoyed by skiers atop "High Cliffs" at the west end of South Rim Trail.

The **CUT ACROSS TRAIL** (.6 mile) follows an easy route over a low ridge that joins the east end of the Magnetic Rock Trail and Warrens Road with the trailhead at Borderland Lodge.

The **BRICE BREON TRAIL** (2.8 miles) connects the public landing at Loon Lake with the middle of the South Rim Trail. An intermediate-level trail, it basically descends from east to west, and has not been groomed in past years.

The **LONELY LAKE TRAIL** (2.5 miles) lies just north of and parallels the South Rim Trail. An intermediate-level trail, it has not been groomed in the past, but will be in future years. Currently, it is a good route for snowshoers to test their talent.

The **NORTH STAR TRAIL** (4 miles) is the newest addition to the Gunflint Lake Area Trails. It connects the southeast corner of the Ham Lake Trail with the Banadad Artery Trail, at a point .7 mile south of the Gunflint Trail. This is an excellent intermediate-level route that passes over numerous small hills and through a variety of forest habitats. Nature photographers should keep their cameras handy, as this area is frequented by moose.

FOR MORE INFORMATION: Contact the Gunflint Ranger District, United States Forest Service, Grand Marais, MN 55604, or any of the resorts on Gunflint Lake.

LODGING

There are three lodges at the west end of Gunflint Lake: Borderland Lodge, Gunflint Lodge and Heston's Country Store and Cabins. All have direct access to the fine system of groomed trails in the Gunflint Lake area.

GUNFLINT LODGE

OWNER/MANAGER: Bruce and Sue Kerfoot

ADDRESS: Box 100 GT, Grand Marais, MN 55604

PHONE: (218) 388-2294 or Toll Free for Reservations: Instate 1-800-328-3362, Outstate 1-800-328-3325

LODGING: 2-4-bedroom Earth Sheltered Chalets, and private rooms for two to four people in the Hostel building (maximum capacity of 28 guests) Housekeeping or American Plan available.

DINING: Family style meals are available by reservation only.

AMENITIES: Sauna for 8-12 people, kitchen facilities available to all guests, waxing and ski storage room

SPECIAL PROGRAMS: Participates in lodge-to-lodge ski-through program.

COMMENTS: Gunflint Lodge is a friendly, informal resort that has been owned and managed by the Kerfoot family for over 50 years. It rests on the very edge of the Laurentian Divide, where scenic bluffs, lovely lakes and tranquil valleys are no more than a kick and glide away from the rooms.

The beautiful Earth Sheltered Chalets provide deluxe accommodations, each with two baths, a living room with fireplace, a full kitchen, carpeting and a view of the lake. The Hostel building offers less expensive accommodations in private rooms, each with a sink and toilet. Two tub/shower rooms are shared by all. On the lower level is a cozy den with fireplace and a large kitchen-dining room that guests may also share. Since the Hostel can comfortably accommodate up to 20 people, it is an ideal facility for ski clubs, large groups and family reunions.

Beautiful earth-sheltered chalets provide deluxe accommodations for guests at Gunflint Lodge.

119

BORDERLAND LODGE

OWNER/MANAGER: Jim and Nancy Thompson

ADDRESS: Box 102 GT, Grand Marais, MN 55604

PHONE: (218) 388-2233

LODGING: Four 2-4-bedroom "Cedar Hus" cabins, and 2 2-bedroom "Villa" units above the main lodge: Housekeeping or American Plan available.

DINING: Meals are available by reservation only.

AMENITIES: Sauna, waxing room, fireplace in the lodge and in all Cedar Hus units; gift shop and grocery store.

SPECIAL PROGRAMS: Lodge-to-lodge ski trips available.

COMMENTS: Borderland Lodge sits no more than a snowball's throw from the Canadian border at the northern end of the splendid Gunflint Lake ski trails. All of the lodging accommodations are fully furnished for housekeeping, have private baths and overlook Gunflint Lake. The Cedar Hus cabins offer deluxe accommodations, carpeted, with Earth Stoves — airtight wood heaters that convert into fireplaces. All guests may, by reservation, enjoy an occasional meal in the Voyageur View dining room.

HESTON'S COUNTRY STORE AND CABINS

OWNER/MANAGER: Chuck and Sharlene Gecas

ADDRESS: SG 50, Grand Marais, MN 55604

PHONE: (218) 388-2243

LODGING: 6 housekeeping cabins each accommodate 2-7 people; choice of rustic (sans water) or modern (with showers, hot and cold water).

AMENITIES: Large wood-burning sauna

SPECIAL PROGRAMS: New Year's Celebration, with bonfire, sing-along, hot cider and buffet.

COMMENTS: Heston's Country Store and Cabins is a small, quiet low-key resort that caters to cross-country skiing, snowshoeing and ice fishing. It offers a viable alternative to vacationers who prefer to save their money by staying in rustic cabins without running water, heated by wood stoves and equipped for housekeeping. But modern cabins are also available, where hot showers are possible. All guests are invited to enjoy the large, wood-burning sauna perched right on the shore of Gunflint Lake.

Heston's Country Store and Cabins sit right on the shore of beautiful Gunflint Lake.

At Heston's Cabins, guests are treated to a steaming hot sauna after a day of skiing . . . followed by a refreshing plunge through a hole in the ice.

The Northwoods Ski Trail is known by few people outside of Silver Bay.

CHAPTER 6

HEART OF THE ARROWHEAD REGION

The southeastern part of Lake County is a lovely and peaceful region through which State Highway 1 connects the North Shore with the Ely area. The only population centers are the tiny towns of Finland and Isabella, where there are grocery stores, service stations, restaurants and bars. Outside of the town, population is sparse and winter resorts are few and far between. Consequently the ski trails in this area offer good opportunities to escape from the winter crowds.

Currently, there are nearly 45 miles of groomed ski trails in the Finland-Isabella area. In addition, there are two state parks (Tettegouche and George H. Crosby Manitou) that are grouped in this guide with the North Shore State Parks, although they are also situated in the Heart of the Arrowhead. The Suomi Nordic Ski Club has proposed an extensive network of trails that would connect these two state parks with dozens of miles of additional trails and link to the North Shore Trail.

For an update on that trail system, or for general information about the Heart of the Arrowhead region, contact: Heart of the Arrowhead, P.O. Box 578, Finland, MN 55603.

Northwoods Ski Trail

Use Level: Moderate

Trail Type: Groomed and single-tracked

Difficulty: Beginner and Intermediate

Trail Length: 9.3 miles

Connects To: Tettegouche State Park

Maps: Available from the Northwoods Ski Touring Club

Highlights: Lovely riverside setting

Trailhead: 1.6 miles west of Silver Bay, via County Road 5 (Penn Blvd.). A parking lot is adjacent to the highway.

Description: This lovely little network of trails is probably known by few people outside of the Silver Bay-Finland area. Those who have discovered it, however, give it high ratings. Nestled along the banks of the East Branch of the Beaver River, the trails loop north to Cedar Creek and west to Bean Lake. A snowmobile trail passes through the middle of the system, but none of the trails is shared.

The hardwood forest through which the trails pass is dominated by aspen and birch, with some balsam fir. The landscape is gently rolling. Sightings of big game are not common in this area, but skiers may have an opportunity to see snowshoe hares, pine martens, fishers and wintering birds.

80% of the trail system is suitable for inexperienced skiers. No expert skills are necessary on any of the loops. Single tracks are groomed throughout the narrow, winding trails, and most of the loops are designed for 1-way traffic. Intersections are clearly marked with "you are here" signs. Near the top of the northernmost loop is the junction of a fairly easy connecting trail leading to Tettegouche State Park, 3.7 miles northeast of the Northwoods Ski Trail. Though easy, it is rated "intermediate" by trail coordinators because of the distance involved.

Intermediate skiers will find the greatest challenge at the center of the system, where the trail climbs to an overlook on a rock outcropping. The entire Northwoods network can be skied easily by intermediates in less than three hours. By extending the route to Tettegouche Park, however, there is plenty of skiing for anyone to fill a whole day.

FOR MORE INFORMATION: Contact the Northwoods Ski Touring Club, P.O. Box 52, Silver Bay, MN 55614. Or call Sawtooth Mountain Lodge for lodging information and current snow conditions: (218) 353-7316.

A guest book is used to register skiers using the Northwoods Ski Trail.

Flathorn-Gegoka Ski-Touring Area

Use Level: Moderate

Trail Type: Machine groomed and track-set

Difficulty: Beginner and Intermediate

Trail Length: 15 miles

Maps: Available at National Forest Lodge on Lake Gegoka or Isabella Ranger Station six miles east of the trailhead.

Highlights: Easier trails for beginning skiers through an interesting variety of forest habitats; no "serious" hills; Many deer!

Trailhead: The Flathorn-Gegoka Ski Trail system is located about midway between Ely and Lake Superior, just west of Isabella, along State Highway 1. Parking is available at either the Lake Gegoka Public Boat Access, 32 miles southeast of Ely, or at National Forest Lodge, ½ mile closer to Ely. There is no fee for parking, or for trail use.

Description: Primarily following a network of logging roads, this ski trail system consists of 15 miles of well-groomed trails. All trails are clearly marked with plastic diamonds and each intersection contains a numbered post and a marked map. The most heavily used trails, situated closest to National Forest Lodge, are double-tracked. The rest are single-tracked. Beginners can ski for miles without encountering any steep hills or treacherous corners. For intermediate skiers more challenging trails extend to the northern extremes of the trail system. Although there are no prominent overlooks that afford panoramic vistas, the variety of forest habitat provides an interesting setting for skiers — especially those being introduced to the North Woods winter.

There is a vast network of interconnected loops extending from the south side of Lake Gegoka northeast to Flathorn Lake and the Little Isabella River and northwest nearly to Gander Lake. Motorized use of the entire area is prohibited during the winter (except for a small section of trail near the Little Isabella River that utilizes a plowed logging road). The only part of the trail system that may not be trackset by a grooming machine is across Lake Gegoka from the public access.

The easiest and most popular trail leads north on a logging road and is double tracked. Even the most inexperienced skiers will have no difficulty negotiating this stretch in an hour and a half or less. Single track trails extend to the east of this "corridor trail" toward Flathorn Lake and along the Little Isabella River. These loops are hilly and more appropriate for an intermediate skier.

More single-tracked trails extend northwest of the "corridor trail." Those closest to Lake Gegoka are also quite level and should pose no problems for a beginner, although a few small hills will be encountered. Recent logging has occurred in some of this area. You'll witness forest management practices, as you ski through some areas that have been clear-cut very recently, while, in other areas, stands of large pines have been thinned. You'll have an excellent opportunity to see deer in this region, as they yard here in the winter. You may also see evidence of wolves and moose.

In this region, a novice skier may easily ski through several forest habitats: dense stands of mature balsam fir, jack pine and spruce, to open spruce bogs and cattail swamps, to a thick stand of young aspens, through wetlands containing cedar, and then back into a mature stand of impressive white pines near the northwest shore of Lake Gegoka.

Trail loops extending further northwest pass through stands of large Norway pine and regenerating forest. Recommended for at least intermediate skiers, these loops are hilly, with some steep downgrades and corners. A trail shelter hut has been constructed at intersection #26, where skiers may wish to enjoy a mid-day rest and warming. Skiers should allow at least three hours (more for inexperienced beginners) for a loop through the northwestern extremes of this trail system.

With National Forest Lodge located on the south side of Lake Gegoka and the Environmental Learning Center situated just south of Flathorn Lake, this ski system is generally well used and well maintained.

FOR MORE INFORMATION: Contact the Isabella District Ranger, P.O. Box 27, Isabella, MN 55607. Or call (218) 323-7722 for current snow conditions.

The remote Woodland Caribou Trail.

Woodland Caribou Trail

Use Level: Light

Trail Type: Natural Environment; not machine groomed and track-set

Difficulty: Intermediate

Trail Length: 20 miles

Maps: Brochure with map available from the Area Forest Supervisor, 6163 Rich Lake Road, Duluth, MN 55803, or at the trailhead.

Highlights: Level terrain

Trailhead: On the west side of Lake County Highway #2, 38 miles north of Highway 61 in Two Harbors. This is 8 miles south of Highway 1.

Description: Situated in the northwest corner of Finland State Forest, the Woodland Caribou ski touring area includes 20 miles of trails on nearly level terrain. Two large loops are accessed by a 3-mile spur trail leading west from the parking area next to Highway 2. The largest loop extends more than 11 miles around several small lakes, with a 1.3-mile spur trail leading to the west shore of Lobo Lake. Combined with two trips across the access trail from the parking lot, completion of this loop requires more than 17 miles of skiing — too long a day for inexperienced skiers.

A shorter loop encircles Bonga Lake — a total distance of 10½ miles round-trip from the parking lot. It is because of the distance involved that this trail system is rated moderately difficult. Only strong and experienced skiers should attempt routes in excess of 10 miles that have not been previously tracked.

Because of the nearly level terrain, there is only one scenic overlook along the entire 20-mile trail network. For those who tackle the largest loop, a shelter hut sits near the westernmost end of the loop.

This area was one of the last strongholds of woodland caribou in Minnesota. They no longer inhabit the region, but Finland State Forest is home for a substantial population of moose, white-tailed deer and timber wolves. Fishers, bobcats and ruffed grouse are also common species that frequent the forest.

FOR MORE INFORMATION: Contact the Area Forest Supervisor, 6163 Rice Lake Road, Duluth, MN 55803. Or phone (218) 723-4669 for current snow conditions.

Deer thrive in the logged region around the Flathorn-Gegoka Ski Area.

Other Skiing Opportunities In The Heart of the Arrowhead Region

In the region between Isabella and the southern border of the Boundary Waters Canoe Area is a vast network of Forest Routes and old logging roads that are not currently being used during the winter months. In fact, the only road in the region that IS normally plowed is the Trappers Road (Forest Route 369) that extends north from Isabella. Other roads MAY be plowed, if logging operations are underway. But that will vary from year to year.

By using these roads, skiers have an excellent opportunity to escape from other people via relatively easy routes over gently sloping hills and few sharp corners. Wildlife sightings are likely, since animals also like to follow these roads. Maps can be obtained from the Forest Service. And one of the rangers can inform you about the current status of plowed roads.

Powwow Lake Hiking Trail

Straight north of Isabella, Forest Route 377 ends at a parking area just south of Isabella Lake. That marks the southern border of the BWCAW and the beginning of an extensive system of hiking trails called the Powwow Lake Hiking Trail — over 50 miles in all. Unfortunately, after several snowfalls, it is highly unlikely that you can drive to the trailhead, since the roads leading there are not usually plowed. Nevertheless, for those looking for an extended winter camping experience, this area could be just the ticket. It may take a day of skiing just to get TO the trail system, and another day to get back to your car. But, after you've arrived, you should have the wilderness to yourself — except for a large population of moose, that is.

The hiking trails were designed, largely, to follow an existing system of old logging roads that were abandoned when this region was incorporated into the BWCAW. The west end of the system, however, was cut just for hikers. The trail goes through a variety of landscapes ranging from stands of virgin timber to very young seedlings. There are boggy lowlands, rolling hills, rock ledges overlooking lakes and more. An excellent map and brochure explaining the trail system is available at the Isabella Ranger Station.

Hogback Lake Hiking Trail

This 5-mile trail is accessible from Co. Rd. 7 near Alger Lake, north of Finland, MN. The name "Hogback" refers to the long, sharply crested ridge that forms part of the Laurentian Divide. The ridgetop trail between Hogback and Scarp lakes offers spectacular views of the lakes and surrounding landscape. Other parts of the trail skirt the bottom of ridges, where rock walls tower 60 to 70 feet high.

Because of the rugged terrain, this trail is recommended only for advanced skiers who are seeking a challenge. Ski with caution! A brochure that includes a map of the trail may be acquired at the Isabella Ranger Station.

The Flathorn-Gegoka Ski Touring Area offers superbly groomed trails that utilize a vast network of old logging roads — ideal for beginning skiers.

A warming hut near the north end of Flathorn-Gegoka trails is a popular destination for skiers.

HEART OF THE ARROWHEAD LODGING

The Heart of the Arrowhead is a sparsely populated region stretching along Highway 1 from the Finland area to the Isabella area. There are few businesses that cater to cross country skiers. For that reason, it is a fine area in which to escape from the crowds.

SAWTOOTH MOUNTAIN LODGE

OWNER/MANAGERS: Carol Lund and Gary Swapinski
ADDRESS: 34 Birch Lane, Silver Bay, MN 55614
PHONE: (218) 353-7316
LODGING: 3 housekeeping log cabins
AMENITIES: Sauna
COMMENTS: Sawtooth Mountain Lodge is a small, cozy and comfortable resort that caters exclusively to cross-country skiers. Resting in a beautiful stand of mature pine on the scenic shore of Lax Lake, at the edge of Tettegouche State Park, this peaceful lodge is an ideal place to really "get away from it all." The philosophy of the new owners is to share their beautiful piece of the Northwoods with others who can appreciate it, too. Although the lodge has had a long and rather intriquing history (built by a "syndicate" man from Minneapolis and visited by the likes of Al Capone) it has only recently been renovated into a resort facility. A short access trail connects the lodge with Tettegouche Park and on to the Northwoods Trail.

Sawtooth Mountain Lodge caters exclusively to cross country skiers.

National Forest Lodge, overlooking Lake Gegoka, serves as a main anchor for the Flathorn-Gegoka Ski Touring Area.

NATIONAL FOREST LODGE
OWNER/MANAGER: Bob Hunger
ADDRESS: 3226 Hwy 1, Isabella, MN 55607
PHONE: (218) 323-7676
LODGING: Cabins to accommodate families or large groups, and 3-bedroom luxury condominium units with full kitchens, baths and fireplaces.
DINING: American Plan meals served family style in large dining room.
AMENITIES: Sauna, central showers and washrooms
COMMENTS: National Forest Lodge sits on the south shore of Lake Gegoka, about midway between Finland and Ely on Highway 1. It serves as the main anchor for the Flathorn-Gegoka Ski Touring Area. National Forest Lodge has long been a popular destination among skiers from the Twin Cities. The flat to gently rolling terrain surrounding the lodge is particularly well-suited for beginning skiers and others who have no propensity for fast downhill runs. The lodge has instructors available and will provide shuttle service to remote trails leading into the Boundary Waters Wilderness.

SNOW TRAILS
OWNER/MANAGER: Lloyd Gilbertson
ADDRESS: 130 County Road 7, Finland, MN 55603
PHONE: (218) 353-7744
LODGING: Wilderness tent camping
COMMENTS: High adventure winter travel by dogsled, skis and snowshoes has been Snow Trails business since 1979. Groups of 4 to 10 people take cross-country trips of 3 to 8 days into the Boundary Waters Wilderness or along the North Shore Trail. They normally camp in wall tents with wood stoves, though sometimes snow shelters are employed. For Northwoods visitors who consider resorts too confining, but who aren't quite ready to strike out on their own, Snow Trails offers a great opportunity to learn the techniques essential for winter camping.

CHAPTER 7

THE ELY AREA

Ely is a small town in the north-central part of the Arrowhead, buried deep in the heart of Superior National Forest and sitting on the edge of the Boundary Waters Canoe Area Wilderness. Known throughout the country as the Canoe Capitol of America, Ely is less known for its exceptional list of diverse winter sports activities — dog sledding, ski jumping, snowshoeing, snowmobiling and cross country skiing. A world-class 60-meter ski jump is the site for international competitions each winter. The Ely All-American Dog Sled Championships take place each January on a course near the outskirts of town. There is a host of snowmobile trails throughout Superior National Forest. But the Northwoods tranquility of the Boundary Waters Canoe Area Wilderness is reserved strictly for skiers and snowshoers.

There are many locations at which one may begin a wilderness journey into the Boundary Waters. Literally hundreds of frozen lakes and streams and snow-covered portage trails — routes that have been used for hundreds of years by Chippewa Indians, French-Canadian Voyageurs and contemporary canoeists — provide potential routes for cross country skiers who prefer to strike out on their own, breaking their own trails as they go.

For skiers who would rather stick to designated ski trails, there are more than 65 miles of routes from which to choose in the Ely area. Two-thirds of that mileage is machine groomed and track-set. In addition, there are 130 miles of wilderness trails nearby, accessible from County Road 116, connecting the Ely and Crane Lake areas. (See chapter 8: The Echo Trail Region). The number and length of Nordic ski trails have grown markedly over the past few years, and construction is currently underway on more trails to support the growing number of winter resort facilities.

Ely is a modern, bustling community with supermarkets, motels, restaurants, laundromats, service stations and a variety of specialty and department stores to serve the tourist community. Ski rentals are available at Voyageur North Outfitters, at the east edge of town. A very nice airport is located about five miles south of town. For information about Ely and the surrounding area, contact the Ely Chamber of Commerce, 1600 E. Sheridan Street, Ely, MN 55731.

Maps for trails in the Ely area and the Echo Trail region are available at the Ely Chamber of Commerce log cabin.

A skier finds the best vantage point to view the Ely All-American Dog Sled races near Ely in January.

Hidden Valley Ski Area is best known for its world-class 60-meter ski jump.

The hilly course at Hidden Valley Ski Area is ideal for intermediate-level skiers.

Hidden Valley Recreation Area

Use Level: Moderate

Difficulty: Mostly intermediate

Trail Type: Machine Groomed and Track-set

Trail Length: 11.2 miles

Connects to: Taconite State Trail

Maps: Available from the Ely Chamber of Commerce, or at Hidden Valley.

Highlights: Equipment rental shop, food service and flush toilets at trailhead, open weekends and holidays.

Trailhead: 2 miles east of Ely. From the Chamber of Commerce Building at the east edge of town (junction of Highways 1 and 169), drive east for ½ mile to the Hidden Valley road. Turn right and drive 1 mile to the recreation area.

Description: Hidden Valley is a municipal recreation area owned and operated by the City of Ely. The trailhead is also the site of an Alpine ski slope and a 60-meter Olympic Ski Jump that attracts competitors from all over the world. The World Cup Nordic Combined events will be hosted by Ely at Hidden Valley during the winter of 1986-87. Don't worry if you find the parking lot cluttered with cars; crowds aren't likely to be found on the cross country ski trails.

Four trails combine to form several loops in the hilly, wooded region just east of the recreation center. A large map sits at the entrance to the trails, but the trail junctions are not well-marked. Those who don't pay close attention to the various trail options could easily get disoriented. The most common error seems to occur by skiing right past the ski trails on the multiple-use trail that follows the power line running east from Hidden Valley. Large arrows are situated to direct traffic, but, unfortunately, the arrows don't tell skiers **where** they are going. If you put your trust in the arrows, you'll eventually find yourself back at the trailhead.

Most of the trails are a bit too challenging for beginning skiers. People with more experience, however, will surely enjoy the rolling landscape and scenic forest enviroment. All of the loops can be easily negotiated in less than 1½ hours by competent skiers.

FOR MORE INFORMATION: Contact the Ely Chamber of Commerce, 1600 E. Sheridan Street, Ely, MN 55731. Or call (218) 365-6123 for current snow conditions.

South Farm Lake Trails

Use Level: Light

Trail Type: Mostly machine groomed and track-set

Difficulty: Beginner to Intermediate

Trail Length: 6.8 miles

Maps: Available from the Kawishiwi District Ranger or the Chamber of Commerce in Ely

Highlights: One of the best groomed trails in the Ely area; Easy terrain for beginners.

Trailhead: 7½ miles east of Ely on County Road 16. From the Chamber of Commerce building in Ely, drive east for 1½ miles to the junction of County Roads 58 and 16. Turn right and follow St. Louis County Road 58, which after one mile turns into Lake County Road 16, for six miles to the parking lot at Superior Forest Lodge.

Description: This fine trail system is perfect for less experienced skiers who prefer to ski on some of the best groomed trails in the Ely area. Most of the system is within the Boundary Waters Canoe Area Wilderness, where the trails may be used only by skiers and where one may quickly escape to a high-quality wilderness experience. Besides the groomed trails, there are other opportunities for the adventurous skier to "break trail" to more remote parts of the wilderness area.

One of the trails crosses South Farm Lake and the east end of Farm Lake. Skiers must, therefore, be wary of hazardous ice conditions when crossing those lakes.

The trails emanating from Superior Forest Lodge form a large figure-eight pattern, and they may be skied in either direction. Skiing overland first, the route follows a multiple-use trail from County Road 16 southeast to a bridge crossing the southern tip of South Farm Lake. Just beyond the bridge, the trail splits. The multiple-use trail branches off toward the south, while the groomed **BRIDGE RUN** (2¼ miles) enters the Boundary Waters Wilderness and leads northeast across a gently rolling landscape to intersect the Spruce-Muskeg Trail.

Bridge Run crosses a delightfully rolling landscape covered with spruce, birch and aspen.

Skiers cross a large muskeg swamp at the east end of the Spruce-Muskeg Trail.

The **SPRUCE-MUSKEG TRAIL** (2½ miles) forms a large loop east of South Farm Lake, following old roads part of the way. The east end of the loop crosses a large muskeg swamp. This part of the trail is not groomed, and skiers may feel as though they are exploring the sub-arctic tundra. This is the only part of the trail system that is not single-tracked and machine groomed.

Back at the intersection with the Bridge Run, skiers may now enjoy the only significant downhill run in the system — a 60-foot drop down a long hill to South Farm Lake. The trail then continues westbound, across South Farm Lake to the trailhead at the east side of Farm Lake.

FOR MORE INFORMATION: Contact the Kawishiwi District Ranger, United States Forest Service, 118 South 4th Avenue East, Ely, MN 55731, or Superior Forest Lodge. Or call the lodge for lodging information and current snow conditions.

Bridge run.

SUPERIOR FOREST LODGE

OWNER/MANAGER: Nancy and Tim Krugman
ADDRESS: Star Route 1, Box 3199, Ely, MN 55731
PHONE: (218) 365-4870
LODGING: 1-3 bedroom housekeeping cabins, without running water.
AMENITIES: Sauna, recreation room with color T.V., games, fireplace and an old time piano; ski rentals
COMMENTS: Superior Forest Lodge is a charming resort on the southeast shore of Farm Lake — the anchor for the South Farm Lake Ski Trail. Seven cabins are equipped for housekeeping. Although the water is turned off in winter, each cabin is supplied with a porta-potty, and a fresh supply of water is provided each day. Showers and sauna are located in a central facility near the lodge. Groomed ski trails begin right outside the lodge.

Superior Forest Lodge is a charming resort on the southeast shore of Farm Lake.

Jasper Hills Trails

Use Level: Light

Trail Type: Mostly machine-groomed and track-set

Difficulty: Mostly intermediate, some beginner and advanced

Trail Length: 14.5 miles

Maps: Available from the Kawishiwi District Ranger or the Chamber of Commerce office in Ely, or at Northwind Lodge.

Highlights: Nice blend of skiing terrain; good wildlife area; One of only a few trails in the Ely area that are machine groomed and track-set

Trailhead: At Tofte or Jasper lake accesses, approximately 14 miles east of Ely. From the Chamber of Commerce building in Ely, drive east on Highway 169. After 4 miles, this road becomes County Road 18 (the Fernberg Road). Continue for ten more miles to the Tofte Lake parking area on the right (south) side of the road. ½ mile further is the entrance to Northwind Lodge on Jasper Lake, where food and toilet facilities are available to skiers and where one may also park and gain access to the trail system.

Description: Completed in the fall of 1984, this beautiful trail system is the newest in the Ely area, and it promises to be one of the best. One of only three systems in the Ely area that offers groomed and tracked trails for skiers, there are plans underway to make Jasper Hills an anchor for a much larger system of trails that may extend all the way east to Lake One, at the end of the Fernberg Road, connecting the Jasper Hills area with the Flash Lake and Fernberg Tower trails. Construction has begun, but it has a ways to go. Nevertheless, Jasper Hills is, by itself, a great little system that will challenge and delight skiers in the Ely area.

A multiple-use trail along the north side of the Fernberg Road that connects Fall and Moose lakes runs through the middle of this system. So it is possible to share the trail with snowmobiles. But it receives only light use, and encounters with snowmobiles are unlikely. The rest of the system is designed and maintained strictly for skiers, using trails that are machine groomed and track-set. The trails cross an interesting blend of hilly woodlands, creek-side marshes, cedar swamps and frozen lake surfaces. Although skiers have an opportunity to experience the feeling of remote wilderness skiing, they don't have to ski far to find it. The trails were well designed for skiers, and minimum development was emphasized to not detract from the beautiful wilderness setting. Skiers are not likely to see many other people, but wildlife sightings are common. There are plenty of moose and deer in the area, and skiers may also view otters and mink. Forest habitats vary from white pine, aspen and balsam fir on the hills to black spruce and cedar in the wetter lowlands. Since most of the trails cross lakes, be cautious of the ice conditions.

The **CEDAR SWAMP LOOP** (1¼ miles) is considered a good warm-up trail through an exquisite stand of cedar trees. The trail begins at the parking area for Northwind Lodge and leads southeast to the swampland. It's an easy route with gently sloping downhill runs that beginners should have no trouble negotiating. This is the only trail that is not directly connected with the rest of the system.

The **JASPER CREEK LOOP** (2.3 miles) begins at the south shore of Jasper Lake (Northwind Lodge) and leads northeast to the northeast corner of the lake. At the point where Jasper Creek drains the lake, the trail climbs a small hill, and then there is a long downhill run to the wide creek valley below. The trail then follows the south shore of Jasper Creek for about 1 kilometer to an intersection with the Enchanted Lake Loop, where there is a short, but steep hill that may necessitate the removal of your skis. The southbound trail leading across Enchanted Lakes to the north shore of Jasper Lake returns to the trailhead at Northwind Lodge. The overland part of this loop is recommended for intermediate skiers.

The **ENCHANTED LAKES LOOP** (2.4 miles) is a nice combination of skiing on lakes and the hilly woodlands just west of Jasper Lake. The loop begins in the middle of Jasper Lake, straight north of Northwind Lodge, and it can be skied as easily in either direction. Skiing counterclockwise, the trail first leads to the north end of Jasper Lake where there is a short overland trail leading to the Enchanted Lakes. At the east end of the northermost lake, the trail leads west from an intersection with the Jasper Creek Trail and loops southwest over a number of hills to the west end of Jasper lake. Recommended for intermediate skiers, this is probably the most beautiful of the Jasper Hills Trails. The loop passes through stands of tall cedars, tamarack and white ash. At times the secluded trail is bordered on both sides by cliffs.

The **MOOSE LAKE LOOP** (2 miles) is an extension of the Jasper Creek Loop. Just before the trail drops down to the creek, the Moose Lake Trail spurs off to the northeast and loops through the southwest end of Moose Lake. At the northwest tip of the lake, the trail again follows Jasper Creek, until it intersects with the Jasper-Tofte Lakes loop. Although most of the trail is on lakes and creek meadows, it is recommended for intermediate skiers. Be cautious of poor ice conditions.

The **JASPER-TOFTE LAKES LOOP** (3.7 miles) contains the only part of the system that is recommended for advanced skiers. It is also the only trail that was originally constructed for snowmobile use, but there is very little use now. Because of the steep hills on the route, it is suggested that skiers travel in a counter-clockwise direction. The eastern part of the loop shares the route of the Enchanted Lakes Loop. But this trail veers north from Enchanted Lakes to follow Jasper Creek. It then heads southwest and surmounts a big hill en route to the northeast end of Tofte Lake. About a half kilometer down the east shoreline of the lake, the trail then turns eastward and climbs another steep hill before rejoining the Enchanted Lakes Loop and returning to the southwest end of Jasper Lake.

The **TOFTE LAKE-ROOKIE POND TRAIL** (1.5 miles) intersects the west end of the Jasper-Tofte Loop. From there it leads west across Tofte Lake and a short downhill connecting trail to Rookie Pond, and ends at the Wood Lake portage. At that point, skiers may opt to continue on the half-mile downhill trail to Wood Lake. But this is not maintained as part of the Jasper Hills system.

The **DISCOVERY LAKE TRAIL** (3.5 miles) leads east from the Cedar Swamp Loop and crosses a rolling landscape en route to Discovery Lake. This is the first phase of the network of connecting trails that will join Jasper Hills with Flash Lake and the Fernberg Tower trails. Most of the trail is suitable for inexperienced skiers, but there are a few downhill runs that

The Discovery Lake Trail serves as a connecting link between the Jasper Hills and Flash Lake trails.

will add excitement to the course. The trail crosses a couple of plowed roads. Exercise caution at those points. This trail may reach all the way to the Flash Lake network by the winter of 1986-87. Contact Northwind Lodge or the Kawishiwi Ranger District in Ely for progress reports.

FOR MORE INFORMATION: Contact the Kawishiwi District Ranger, USFS, 118 S. 4th Avenue East, Ely, MN 55731, or Northwind Lodge. Or call the lodge for lodging information or current snow conditions.

Northwind Lodge overlooks Jasper Lake.

NORTHWIND LODGE
OWNER/MANAGER: The Joe Baltich family
ADDRESS: P.O. Box 690, Ely, MN 55731
PHONE: (218) 365-5489
LODGING: Modern deluxe housekeeping cabins, some with running water in winter
AMENITIES: Sauna, central shower building, complete toilet facilities
COMMENTS: Located on the south shore of Jasper Lake, and serving as a trailhead for the Jasper Hills Trail, Northwind Lodge is a brand new addition to the winter lodging facilities that are available in the Ely area. 1, 3 and 4-bedroom cabins are equipped for housekeeping, though only one cabin is completely winterized, with running water, hot shower and flush toilet. The other cabins are winterized and have access to the central shower building, and all guests are welcome in the Finnish sauna. Northwind Lodge plans to increase its winter accommodations right along with the growth of the splendid trail system that surrounds it. Staple groceries, hot sandwiches, pizza and pop are now available at the lodge, and plans call for a restaurant in the future. Skiers will enjoy the friendly hospitality of the Baltich family.

Fernberg Tower Trails

Use Level: Light

Trail Type: Natural environment; not groomed and tracked

Difficulty: Mostly intermediate

Trail Length: 12.4 miles

Maps: Available from the Kawishiwi Ranger District or the Chamber of Commerce in Ely.

Highlights: An unmarked Boundary Waters Wilderness trail, often with unbroken snow

Trailhead: At the Lake One Landing 20 miles east of Ely. From the Chamber of Commerce building, drive east on Highway 169 (which turns into the Fernberg Road) all the way to its end at a large parking area adjacent to Lake One.

Description: This is a beautiful, though undeveloped, trail system that provides skiers with a delightful variety of Northwoods terrain: rivers, lakes, forest trails and old logging roads. The trails are not too difficult; but, since they are not likely to be tracked by other skiers, the unbroken snow may be a challenge to inexperienced skiers. The southern half of the system is in the Boundary Waters Canoe Area Wilderness, mostly along the Kawishiwi River, between Lake One and Triangle Lake. Although travel permits are not required during the winter, other regulations are in effect year-round. If you follow the river route, for instance, be sure to leave your cans and bottles at home.

Lately, the trail has not been groomed or signed but the Forest Service has plans to incorporate the Fernberg Tower Trails into a much larger network, connecting the Jasper Hills Trails and the Flash Lake Trails. It will be a groomed and tracked system that will afford skiers several days of excellent skiing. Stay tuned for further developments!

From the Lake One parking area, skiers have two options: skiing south on Lake One to the Kawishiwi River, or heading west to the inland trails. Skiing the whole loop in a counter-clockwise direction, you'll enjoy the overland route first. It begins on the west side of the Fernberg Road, across from the north end of the parking lot. The trail leads from there to the old Fernberg Road (Forest Route 1544), and then to an intersection in the trail. The left branch leads west, crosses a swamp and enters a pine plantation. The alert skier has a good chance of seeing wildlife in this area.

After about 1½ miles, the trail intersects Forest Route 439. Less experienced skiers (or those short on time) may want to follow this road north to Forest Route 1544. Then loop back toward the east and follow Route 1544 back to the parking lot. About ½ mile after joining Route 1544, you'll encounter two intersections. Bear right at the first and left at the second. The south-bound road at the second intersection leads to the summit of a big hill that once held the Fernberg Lookout Tower. The fire tower has been replaced by a Lake County radio tower.

Beyond the last intersection are two long hills that drop a total of 150 feet, affording skiers a fast downhill run when the snow conditions are conducive to it. Beginners may find more excitement than they bargained for!

More experienced skiers who are ready for a 10-mile loop can continue west-bound and cross Forest Route 439. The trail leads to the east end of Ojibway Lake and follows the south shore west to the short portage to Triangle Lake. At the south end of Triangle Lake another portage trail crosses over a low hill to the Kawishiwi River, which, in turn, leads east back to Lake One and the trailhead. Use extreme caution while skiing on the river, where weak ice or open water is likely in the vicinity of several rapids. The Forest Service recommends that you ski the river with someone who is familiar with it.

FOR MORE INFORMATION: Contact the Kawishiwi Ranger District, United States Forest Service, 118 S. 4th Avenue East, Ely, MN 55731.

Flash Lake Trails

Use Level: Heavy to Moderate

Trail Type: Mostly machine groomed and track-set

Difficulty: Mostly beginner and intermediate

Trail Length: 8 miles

Maps: Available from the Kawishiwi Ranger District, the Chamber of Commerce in Ely, or Charles L. Sommers National High Adventure Base.

Highlights: Good network of groomed trails that offers a variety of loops for all skill levels

Trailhead: At Charles L. Sommers National High Adventure Base (Boy Scouts of America), 20 miles east of Ely. From the Ely Chamber of Commerce Building, drive east on Highway 169, which turns into the Fernberg Road, for 17.7 miles. Turn left (north) onto the Moose Lake Road (#438) and drive 2½ miles to Sommers Base, where there is a large parking area available for skiers.

Description: The Flash Lake trail is one of the busiest systems in the area on weekends. Anchored by the Charles L. Sommers National High Adventure Base, Boy Scouts of America, the trails are used for ski training, snowshoeing, and winter camping programs that attract scouts and other youth groups from all over the country. Survival training is also taught to the U.S. Army. Consequently, there is a good deal of activity here on mid-winter weekends, including winter campgrounds at various locations throughout the area. During the week, however, there are very few other skiers around.

The Forest Service has plans to tie these trails into a much larger system that will connect them with the Jasper Hills Trails, Lake One and the Fernberg Tower area at the end of the Fernberg Road. This will be a vast network of groomed and tracked trails that will provide several days of great skiing for all types of skiers. Until that comes about, the Flash Lake Trails provide a good opportunity alone.

These trails lie just south of the Boundary Waters Canoe Area Wilderness, sandwiched between the Moose Lake Road on the west and Snowbank Lake on the east. The terrain is gently rolling, but there are occasional short, steep hills and a few tight turns. Some of the routes follow old portage trails between lakes, and some utilize old logging roads.

Flash Lake serves as the hub of the system, with irregular spokes leading from it in all directions, providing a maze of loops through a variety of forest habitats, from dense forests to open fields, marshes and frozen lake surfaces.

Most of the trails are relatively easy to moderate in difficulty. Only a few short segments are rated "most difficult."

The portage trail connecting Flash Lake and Snowbank Lake intersects the Snowbank Hiking Trail, which offers more advanced skiers the opportunity of skiing on wilderness trails that are not groomed and tracked (nor designed for skiers). There are some bald ledgerock ridges along the west side of Snowbank Lake that afford scenic views across the lake and into the Boundary Waters Wilderness.

Another secondary trail encircles Blackstone Lake. It offers a moderately difficult route for experienced skiers. Only an expert skier, however, should even **think** of attempting the trail to Ennis Lake. It is very steep in places, and not designed for skiing. But at the end of the trail is a gorgeous overlook from cliffs high above the northwest shore of Ennis Lake. Even experts should approach this trail with caution!

FOR MORE INFORMATION: Contact the Kawishiwi District Ranger, United States Forest Service. 118 S. 4th Avenue East, Ely, MN 55731.

Boy Scout groups from all over the nation come to Flash Lake to sleep in snow caves.

The trail to Secret and Ennis lakes provides an ungroomed alternative for advanced skiers.

A gently rolling landscape surrounds Flash Lake and contains a maze of ski loops through a variety of forest habitats.

Thomas Lake Trail

Use Level: Light

Trail Type: Natural environment; not groomed and tracked

Difficulty: Beginner skills, but Advanced length

Trail Length: 11.2 miles

Maps: Available from the Kawishiwi District Ranger or the Chamber of Commerce in Ely.

Highlights: Lake Trout fishing on Thomas Lake

Trailhead: The public access to Snowbank Lake, 23 miles northeast of Ely. From the Chamber of Commerce building, drive east on Highway 169 (which turns into the Fernberg Road) for 18.3 miles to the Snowbank Lake Road. Turn left and follow this road 3.2 miles to its end at the public landing and parking lot.

Description: The Thomas Lake Trail was constructed to allow "easy" access for ice fishermen seeking lake trout. Except for the first mile across the south end of Snowbank Lake, the trail is entirely in the Boundary Waters Canoe Area Wilderness. Although travel permits are not required during the winter and camping is allowed at locations other than designated campsites, all other BWCAW regulations are still in effect, including the prohibition of cans and bottles used for foods and beverages.

For most skiers, the entire route to Thomas Lake is too long to be completed in just one day. It's a good winter camping destination for those who would like to try their luck at lake trout fishing. Although the trail is used frequently, it may not be well-tracked for skiers, since dog slegs are often used for transportation to the lake.

From the Snowbank Lake access, the trail leads east to a ¼-mile portage connecting Snowbank and Parent lakes. Another ¼-mile trail joins the northeast end of Parent with the west end of Disappointment Lake. From the east end of Disappointment, then, the trail begins a route over creeks, swamps, beaver flowages and the frozen surfaces of small lakes located south of Disappointment Mountain — a big hill that towers more than 300 feet above the lakes. The trail crosses Muzzle and Kobe lakes and then swings southeasterly down to the west end of Thomas Lake.

There are 17 official Forest Service campsites on Thomas Lake, but camping is not restricted to those locations.

FOR MORE INFORMATION: Contact the Kawishiwi District Ranger, United States Forest Service, 118 S. 4th Avenue East, Ely, MN 55731.

The Thomas Lake Trail crosses big Snowbank Lake.

146

Over 4 miles of groomed ski trails wind through the first
pine plantation in Superior National Forest — the Birch
Lake Plantation.

Birch Lake Plantation

Use Level: Moderate

Trail Type: Usually machine groomed and track-set

Difficulty: Beginner to Intermediate

Trail Length: 4.1 miles

Maps: Available from the Kawishiwi District Ranger in Ely.

Highlights: Nice stand of Norway pines

Trailhead: One mile east of Babbitt. From the Chamber of Commerce building in Ely, drive west through the downtown business district to the junction of highways 169 and 21. Turn left and drive south on Highway 21 for 18 miles to the stop sign and "T" intersection with County Road 70. Turn left and drive past the town of Babbitt for 2.9 miles to the Birch Lake Plantation, one mile east of Babbitt. There is a small parking area .2 mile past Forest Road 131, on the left side of the road.

Description: This nice, little ski area is the result of a combined effort of the United States Forest Service, the Minnesota Department of Natural Resources and the City of Babbitt. Part of the trail passes through a 120-acre area that was the first pine plantation in Superior National Forest. It was planted in 1915 and has been thinned out in recent years. The State of Minnesota portion was constructed by Iron Range Resource and Rehabilitation Board funds and local labor in 1982.

The part of the trail system that parallels the county road is designated for "multiple use," where snowmobiles are also permitted to travel. But most of the area is reserved for skiers.

The trail system is a maze of interconnected loops with "you are here" maps at each junction and blue markers along the paths. The area east of Forest Route 131 is generally quite flat, but the areas west of the road are in a slightly hillier area. None of the trails is difficult. Loops of virtually any length are possible. It's a good place for beginners to develop their kick-and-glide techniques through a lovely pine forest.

FOR MORE INFORMATION: Contact the Kawishiwi Ranger District, United States Forest Service, 118 S. 4th Avenue East, Ely, MN 55731.

OTHER ELY AREA LODGING

Several Ely-area resorts are not affiliated directly with any of the designated ski trails included in this guide. All three listed below provide their own ski trails, however, and each is easily accessible to most of the trail systems described.

BEAR ISLAND RESORT

OWNER: Ann and Mike Rice
ADDRESS: P.O. Box 179-C, Ely, MN 55731
PHONE: (218) 827-3396
LODGING: Three housekeeping cabins, one to six bedrooms
DINING: Full-service "Viking Manor" restaurant and bar, open to the public
AMENITIES: Sauna; private ski trails; lodge with big-screen T.V.; major credit cards accepted (American Express, VISA, Mastercard)
COMMENTS: Located about 12 miles south of Ely, via highway 21, Bear Island Resort offers winterized accommodations that are equipped with running water and hot showers. The two smaller cabins (1 and 2 bedrooms) are fully equipped for housekeeping, and the largest (6 bedrooms) cabin is partially equipped. All meals may be enjoyed in the dining room.

3.1 miles of groomed and tracked ski trails weave across the gently rolling 120-acre wooded tract of private land adjacent to the resort. Most of the trail system is easy to intermediate in difficulty, but there is one steep hill that might challenge advanced skiers. The trails are not machine groomed, but a drag is pulled across the course to set a track. There are numerous other trails in the vicinity of Bear Island Lake, including the Taconite Trail, but all are multiple use trails. Nevertheless, there is very little use of the trails, even on weekends. Skiers who prefer perfectly manicured, machine-groomed and tracked trails will probably be happier elsewhere. But, for skiers who enjoy breaking trail and following seldom-used wilderness routes, the Bear Island Lake area offers miles of multiple-use trails from which to choose.

Bear Island Resort's Viking Manor offers fine cuisine for hungry skiers.

149

THE ESCAPE

OWNER/MANAGER: Bill and Joan Cossette
ADDRESS: P.O. Box 147, Ely, MN 55731
PHONE: (218) 827-2665
LODGING: 6 modern housekeeping cabins, accommodations for 2-12 people
DINING: The Captain's Galley Supper Club and Lounge, open to the public
AMENITIES: Private ski trails, sauna
COMMENTS: Situated on the east shore of Bear Island Lake, 10 miles south of Ely on Highway 21, The Escape offers 2-to-4-bedroom cabins that are completely equipped for housekeeping, including running water and hot showers. Guests who would rather not cook may enjoy a delightful dining experience at the main lodge, where there is also a cocktail lounge.

Skiers may utilize ski trails on The Escape's property. Or, there are numerous multiple-use trails including the Taconite Trail in the vicinity of Bear Island Lake that are shared with snowmobiles, and are not groomed and tracked for skiers. Directions and maps are available for ski trails in the BWCAW.

NORTHERNAIR LODGE

OWNER/MANAGER: Alan and Byrdie Mohler
ADDRESS: Star Route 1, Box 1212, Ely, MN 55731
PHONE: (218) 365-4882
LODGING: Completely modern housekeeping cabins, or American Plan
DINING: The Rendezvous Room restaurant, open to the public
AMENITIES: Sauna, lodge, lounge with games and T.V.
COMMENTS: Northernair Lodge has completely modern, winterized log cabins with stone fireplaces — completely equipped for housekeeping. With the recent addition of a new restaurant, however, cooking is not necessary. Located on Mitchell Lake, only 3½ miles south of Ely via Highway 21, the lodge is easily accessible to all of the ski trails in the Ely area. In addition, there is a nature trail on the property, and there is access to the multiple-use Taconite Trail from the portage connecting Mitchell and Twin lakes.

OTHER WINTER ACCOMMODATIONS

The Ely Chamber of Commerce lists the following additional lodging facilities in the Ely Area:

BEAVER LODGE, Star Route 2, Box 8295, Ely, MN 55731 — Burntside Lake

DISABLED VETERANS WILDERNESS RETREAT, Route 1, Ely, MN 55731 — Fall Lake

KAWISHIWI LODGE, P.O. Box 480E, Ely, MN 55731 — Lake One

KOSIR'S MOTEL, 1314 E. Sheridan Street, Ely, MN 55731

MOTEL ELY, 1047 E. Sheridan Street, Ely, MN 55731

SHAGAWA INN, P.O. Box 148, Ely, MN 55731 — Shagawa Lake

SHIG-WAK RESORT, P.O. Box 388, Ely, MN 55731 — Little Long Lake

TIMBER TRAIL RESORT, Star Route 1, Box 3111, Ely, MN 55731 — Farm Lake

WEST GATE MOTEL, 110 North 2nd Avenue West, Ely, MN 55731

CHAPTER 8

THE ECHO TRAIL REGION

County Road 116 — known locally as the Echo Trail — is a rough, winding, gravel (most of the way) "highway" that connects The Ely Area with Voyageur Country. It begins on the north shore of Shagawa Lake, three miles north of Ely, and extends through rugged wilderness terrain for 46 miles to County Road 24 at Kabustasa Lake, nine miles south of Crane Lake. With the Boundary Waters Canoe Area Wilderness on both sides of the road, there are numerous access points along the Echo Trail where skiers may penetrate the pristine wilderness. Among them are twelve designated ski areas with 137 miles of trails for winter enjoyment. With two exceptions, the trails are very lightly used, mostly intermediate in difficulty, and not originally designed for skiers. The exceptions are the North Arm Trails and North Junction Trails, where an elaborate trail network was laid out specifically for skiers of all abilities. They are also the only ones that are directly associated with winter resort facilities, and, as a result, they receive considerably more use.

There are no towns along the Echo Trail. No service stations. No restaurants. And very few resorts that operate during the winter months. The closest communities are Ely at the southeast end, and Buyck near the northwest end of the road. All of the ski trails can be reached within one hour from either community, when weather conditions are favorable to driving.

None of the ski trails in this region is machine groomed and track-set. They are "natural environment" trails. Following a snowfall, skiers may not find any tracks to follow. Many experienced cross country skiers prefer this type of experience. Novice skiers who need or prefer the stability of a machine groomed track, however, may be happier elsewhere. Within a week after a snowfall, most of the trails will be skier tracked. Nevertheless, in regions like this, skiers should always carry a good map and compass to make certain that they do not stray from the designated ski trails.

For more information about the area, contact the United States Forest Service. The southeastern part of the region is included in the Kawishiwi Ranger District, while the northwestern part is in the La Croix Ranger District. The addresses and phone numbers are included with the individual trail descriptions.

Bass Lake Trail

Use Level: Light

Trail Type: Natural environment; not machine-groomed and track-set

Difficulty: Advanced

Trail Length: 5.6 miles

Maps: Available from the Kawishiwi District Ranger or the Chamber of Commerce in Ely.

Highlights: Dry Falls; ledgerock vistas; nice stand of red pine

Trailhead: Six miles north of Ely, along the Echo Trail. From the Chamber of Commerce building in Ely, drive east on Highway 169 for 1 mile to the junction of County Road 88. Turn left and drive 2.3 miles to the beginning of the Echo Trail (County Road 116). The signed trail and parking area are on the right (north) side of the road, three miles northwest of County Road 88.

Description: Bass Lake is, historically, one of the most interesting lakes in the Ely area. Prior to 1925, the surface of Bass Lake was 55 feet higher than it is today, separated from Low Lake by a high ridge of glacial gravel. In 1925, the glacial ridge washed out. In 10 hours, Bass Lake shrank to about half its original size, creating Dry and Little Dry lakes in the place of the original Bass Lake. Parts of this trail cross over what used to be the bottom of Bass Lake. In other places, the trail crosses high, open ledgerock that affords nice overlooks of the Bass Lake area.

This interesting trail starts at the Bass Lake parking lot and makes a large circle around the lake. It starts down the canoe portage trail (shared with snowmobilers and hikers) for 200 yards to an intersection. Skiing the route in a clockwise direction, the left trail then descends steeply to the old lake bottom, crosses a creek, and then climbs a steep hill to a ridge nearly 100 feet above the creek. Switchbacks create hazardous corners that require caution.

The 5.6-mile Bass Lake Trail begins on the downhill portage from the Echo Trail to Bass Lake.

After a mile, the trail drops quickly to cross a creek connecting Dry and Bass lakes, highlighted by Dry Falls. This is one mile from the trail-head. Beyond the bridge, the trail crosses a portage trail, ascends a steep hill, and then drops down into an elegant stand of Norway pines.

After passing a spur trail that leads to a campsite on Bass Lake, the main trail turns toward the northwest and follows the edge of the old lake bottom north of Dry Lake. Veering back toward the northeast, the trail then climbs to the top of a bald ridge that provides skiers with a scenic overlook. The trail then drops more than 100 feet back down to the old lake bottom and follows it to the northeast end of the lake.

The trail crosses the washed out area that was once the glacial ridge separating Bass and Low lakes. At the end of the washout, the trail crosses a bridge and then turns toward the southwest and follows a ridge along the old southeast shore of Bass Lake, back to the portage trail that returns to the parking lot.

This trail was designed for hikers, not skiers. So beware of a narrow path with some steep slopes and sharp turns. Much of the trail follows nearly level to gently rolling terrain. But advanced skiing skills are necessary to get to the easy parts of the trail. The path is extremely rocky, so good snow depth is necessary to enable smooth skiing. Allow plenty of time for this half-day trek.

FOR MORE INFORMATION: Contact the Kawishiwi District Ranger, United States Forest Service, 118 S. 4th Avenue East, Ely, MN 55731.

Hanson Lake Trail

Use Level: Moderate

Trail Type: Multiple-use, not groomed or tracked for skiers

Difficulty: Intermediate

Trail Length: 5 miles

Maps: Available from the Kawishiwi Ranger District or the Chamber of Commerce in Ely.

Highlights: Combination of lake skiing and a logging road

Trailhead: Fenske Lake Campground, 12 miles north of Ely. From the Chamber of Commerce Building in Ely, drive east on Highway 169 for one mile to its intersection with County Road 88. Turn left and drive 2.3 miles to the Echo Trail (County Road 116). Turn right and follow the Echo Trail for 8.4 miles to the Fenske Lake Campground.

Description: This multiple-use trail is a good combination of lakes portage trails and an old logging road. It is used more by snowmobiles than by skiers. So, although the trail may not be tracked, it may at least be packed by snow machines going to Hanson Lake. Beginning skiers should have little difficulty with the eastern half of the loop, between Fenske Campground and Twin Lake. The western half, however, is more difficult, crossing over many hills between Hanson Lake and the Echo Trail.

Skiing in a clockwise direction, you'll first head east from the campground and follow the south shore of Fenske Lake to the Everett Lake portage trail, which leads south to Everett Lake. After crossing Everett Lake, there is a short portage trail leading west to Twin Lake. On the west shore of Twin Lake, about ⅓ mile from the Everett Lake portage, is the beginning of a trail that leads northwest. At the point where the trail joins an old logging road, there is a spur trail leading west to Hanson Lake. The logging road continues north and then bends toward the northeast en route to the Echo Trail, .3 mile south of the trailhead.

Most of the forest through which you'll ski is typically second growth jack pine, red pine and aspen in the area north of Hanson Lake. At the south end of the loop, however, there are still some old trees standing. As always, when skiing on lakes, be extremely cautious of the ice conditions. Slush can be a problem during mid-winter, and weak ice can result during warm spells, as well as at the beginning and end of the skiing season.

FOR MORE INFORMATION: Contact the Kawishiwi Ranger District, United States Forest Service, 118 S. 4th Avenue East, Ely, MN 55731.

Wolf tracks are common along the ski trails in the Echo Trail Region.

North Junction Trails

Use Level: Moderate

Trail Type: Not machine groomed and track-set; but usually skier tracked.

Difficulty: Intermediate, with some Beginner

Trail Length: 9.3 miles

Maps: Available from the Kawishiwi Ranger District or the Chamber of Commerce in Ely.

Highlights: Good wildlife habitat; interesting variety of terrain and forest habitats

Trailhead: At the junction of County Roads 116 and 644. From the Chamber of Commerce Building in Ely, drive east on Highway 169 for one mile to its intersection with County Road 88. Turn left and drive 2.3 miles to the Echo Trail (County Road 116). Turn right and follow the Echo Trail for 9.4 miles to County Road 644, known as the North Arm Road. Parking space is provided on the left side of the road.

Description: This interesting little network of trails is largely the result of logging operations in the area. Timber harvesting produced back country roads that are ideally suited for cross-country skiing. Trails pass over a variety of terrain, from rolling hills covered with second growth jack pine and aspen to lowland swamps and bogs. Openings in the forest created from logging operations enhance wildlife habitat, providing more desirable sources of food for deer (in the smaller openings) and moose (in the larger openings). Consequently, this is a good area to see moose.

Although the trails are not machine groomed and tracked, the system receives a fair amount of use, especially along the trails closest to Camp Widjiwagan (west end of the system). Consequently, the trails are usually skier tracked.

Several loops are possible through a variety of Northwoods terrain. Most are recommended for intermediate-level skiers, but beginners should be able to enjoy parts of the system.

Three trails originate at the trailhead.

The **BEAVER MEADOWS TRAIL** (1 mile) is the easiest of the trails. It heads off in a southwest direction from the trailhead slopes gently downhill and crosses a long beaver meadow. At the west end of the meadow, it loops north to the North Arm Road, where skiers may cross the road and tie in with the Pine Hills Trail.

The **SOUTH TRAIL** (2½ miles) uses Spruce Road to pass through a spruce bog and cross some beaver ponds. Recommended for intermediate skiers, the trail crosses an interesting variety of terrain with varied forest habitats, including an area that was recently logged, where some panoramic views are possible. The trail leads in a southerly direction from the trailhead and then loops back toward the northwest to join the west end of the Beaver Meadows Trail, just after a nice downhill run to the meadow.

The **WIDJI TRAIL** (1 mile) intersects the west end of the Beaver Meadows Trail. It's an intermediate trail that leads west to YMCA Camp Widjiwagan. Respect this private property as you pass through the camp en route to the North Arm Road and the beginning of the Hunch Creek Trail.

The **HUNCH CREEK TRAIL** (2¼ miles) leads north from the North Arm Road, following Hunch Creek to a long, open meadow bordered by high hills on either side. At the north end of the meadow area, the going becomes quite rough. Only experienced skiers with a desire to "bushwhack" should consider proceeding north to Hunch Lake. Others may want to join the Pine Hills Trail, which intersects Hunch Creek at the south end of the long meadow, about ½ mile north of the North Arm Road.

The **PINE HILLS TRAIL** (2½ miles) offers the greatest challenge to more experienced skiers. Beginning on the north side of the North Arm Road, across from the parking lot, this trail winds across rolling hills on old logging roads, with some good downhill runs for excitement. Along the way is an area that was clear-cut by loggers and is now a young aspen plantation. The trail first loops northwest, but then curves back toward the North Arm Road, where there is an access trail connecting it with the Beaver Meadows Trail. From there, it heads northwest again and splits into two loops (red or blue markers) that join again at the top of a ridge. The trail then continues west to join the Hunch Creek Trail, after a fast downhill run into the Hunch Creek meadow.

FOR MORE INFORMATION: Contact the Kawishiwi Ranger District, United States Forest Service, 118 S. 4th Avenue East, Ely, MN 55731.

Windfalls are not uncommon obstacles across any of the "natural environment" trails in the Echo Trail Region.

"You are here" signs mark all intersections on the North Arm Trails.

North Arm Trails

Use Level: Moderate

Trail Type: Not machine groomed and track-set, but usually skier-tracked

Difficulty: Mostly intermediate; some beginner and advanced

Trail Length: 34 miles

Maps: Available from Kawishiwi Ranger District or the Chamber of Commerce in Ely.

Highlights: Good variety of scenic terrain, with some good downhill runs; old stands of virgin pine: many loop options.

Trailhead: The North Arm Trails are located 17 miles northwest of Ely on the North Arm of beautiful Burntside Lake. From the Chamber of Commerce Building in Ely, drive east on Highway 169 for one mile to its intersection with County Road 88. Turn left there and follow this road for 2.3 miles to the Echo Trail (County Road 116). Turn right and follow the Echo Trail for 9.4 miles to the North Arm Road (County Road 644). Drive southwest from there for 3.5 miles to the Coxey/Slim Trail sign, where parking is provided on the right side of the road.

Description: This scenic network of trails is the largest designated ski trail system in the Ely area. They were constructed and are maintained by a combined effort of the U.S. Forest Service, the State of Minnesota, the neighboring YMCA camps and a contingent of volunteers from as far away as the Twin Cities. Weaving in and out of the Boundary Waters Canoe Area Wilderness, the trails are not machine groomed and track-set, in order to provide skiers with a high quality alternative to the groomed systems found elsewhere. Most of the trails, however, are skier-tracked soon after each snowfall. These trails offer a challenge to the skier's skill and an opportunity to be a part of the wilderness.

A good variety of trail loops were designed to accommodate all skill levels for almost any amount of time available. Most of the trail system, however, is most popular with intermediate-level skiers. Generally rolling terrain is accented with occasional steep ridges that either require exhausting climbs or permit fast downhill runs. Some of the routes utilize the frozen lakes surfaces of the Boundary Waters. When crossing lakes, be especially alert to the possibilities of slush or thin ice.

Three trails originate at the trailhead, and all other trails ultimately branch off from these three trails. The **INDIAN ROCK TRAIL** (1 mile) leads northeast from the trailhead to the south end of Slim Lake, following the base of a high rock ridge. Near Slim Lake it joins the Slim Lake Trail, which is a more difficult route to the same destination. The trail is mostly level, with a few minor hills that might add a degree of excitement for inexperienced skiers.

Novice skiers may then ski on Slim Lake, following its east shoreline about ½ mile to a small bay. At the east end of the bay is the beginning of the Slim Lake canoe portage, which follows the edge of a creek on a gently sloping downhill course to Burntside Lake. Be alert to automobile traffic as you glide across the North Arm Road, just before arriving at the lake. The

BURNTSIDE LAKE LOOP (2½ miles) continues along the north shore of the North Arm of Burntside Lake to the beach at Camp Northland. From there, it is about 150 yards up the gently sloping roadway to the trailhead. This entire loop is over 3.8 miles — a nice morning outing for the novice skier.

300-year-old "Sentinels" straddle
the North Star Run.

The **SLIM LAKE TRAIL** (.75 mile) offers intermediate skiers a more challenging route to Slim Lake. Starting at the parking lot, it climbs from the trailhead to a ridge above the Indian Rock Trail. This route is much hillier and affords skiers the opportunity to enjoy some long, downhill runs, before the trail levels off in the swamps just south of Slim Lake. A spur trail to "Old Baldy" leads to a panoramic view of Burntside's North Arm and the "Narrows" joining it with the main part of Burntside Lake.

The **RICE LAKE LOOP** (4.8 miles) provides intermediate skiers with an extended trek into the Boundary Waters Canoe Area Wilderness, primarily on lakes and ageless portage trails. Skiing in a clockwise direction from the south end of Slim Lake, there is a steep hill to climb just west of the lake. The trail then passes by some old "Druid" pines, estimated to be as old as 300 years, en route to an intersection just over one kilometer west of Slim Lake. The Rice Lake Loop then heads toward the northwest through Keneu Lake to Hook Lake. It then loops toward the east and crosses Rice Lake on the way back to Slim Lake. Wilderness lake skiing can be magnificient, but be wary of ice conditions. Trail locations on the lakes have been chosen to avoid known bad ice, but ice conditions change rapidly during warm spells and at either end of the skiing season.

The **NORTH STAR RUN** (2.4 miles) offers a challenging start to even the most experienced skiers. The beginning is hilly. But after an elevation gain of 200 feet, the terrain settles to a gently rolling pattern. Near the beginning, a long gradual slope is decorated with huge, old pines. Known as the "Sentinels," these pine trees are believed to be almost 300 years old. Up in the gently rolling high country, the trail crosses open ledgerock areas and passes through nice stands of Norway pine. Along the way, you'll see intersections with the Barren Ridge Trail and the Lost Lakes Trail, and then the North Star Run ends at the Coxey Pond Trail.

The **BARREN RIDGE TRAIL** (1 mile) leads north from the middle of the North Star Run, crosses an open ridge and then connects with the Rice Lake Loop .7 miles west of Slim Lake. Recommended for intermediate skiers, there is a long downhill run about midway on the trail.

The **LOST LAKES TRAIL** (1.9 miles) offers intermediate skiers a long, downhill route to Coxey Pond. It winds through nice stands of 100-year-old pines, glides between Lost Lakes, and then enters the northeast end of Coxey Pond, before intersecting the Coxey Pond Trail at the southwest end of this lake.

The **COXEY POND TRAIL** (2.5 miles) extends northwest from the junction of the Trolls Bridge Trail and South Road. Skiers may also begin at the North Arm Road, about ¼ mile southwest of the trailhead parking lot. It follows an old logging road that first climbs rather steeply from the North Arm Road, but then passes over gradual slopes that can be easily negotiated even by inexperienced skiers. The steep climb at the beginning, and a few downhill runs along the trail, however, may provide a bit too much challenge for the novice skier. At the southwest end of Coxey Pond the trail intersects two other trails leading to Cummings Lake and Silica Lake.

The **CUMMINGS LAKE LOOP** (4.1 miles) continues westbound on the same old logging road that leads skiers to Coxey Pond to an intersection with the Bog Trail. Then the trail veers toward the northwest and follows the old Cummings Lake fire trail through nice stands of 80-year-old jack pine. There are a couple of fast downhill runs en route to Cummings Lake. From the northeast corner of Cummings, the route carries skiers over the frozen lake to the southeast corner and a creek leading east to Silica Lake. Be alert to weak ice on the creek. In spite of the flat part of the route over Cummings Lake, this loop is recommended for advanced skiers. The whole route from the North Arm Road and back again is over 9 miles, part of which is over challenging hills. For inexperienced skiers, this could be a bit too much to chew!

The **BOG AND KORB CREEK TRAILS** (3.5 miles) are extensions off the Cummings Lake Loop. Level terrain is characteristic of the route, and much of it is on lake surfaces. The Bog Trail cuts across a spruce bog on the route of an old winter road once used by loggers. At the southeast end of Cummings Lake, then, the trail loops west across Cummings and Korb lakes. It then follows Korb Creek northeast to the creek draining Silica Lake, which is the bottom part of the Cummings Lake loop. Most of the loop is quite easy, but the creek portion of the route is rated "more difficult." Otters are sometimes seen in these creeks, so be alert.

The **OLE LAKE LOOP** (3.5 miles) branches off from the Coxey Pond Trail near the junction of the North Star Run. Traveling in a counterclockwise direction, skiers first pass north of Repose Lake on an easy trail before heading southwest to Ole Lake across difficult terrain that is recommended for advanced skiers. There is one long downhill run to the north end of Ole Lake, followed by a steep climb leading east from the lake. Much of the trail is on pine covered ridges that afford skiers some nice views of the surrounding countryside.

The **TROLLS BRIDGE RUN** (.6 mile) connects the North Star Run to the south end of the Coxey Pond Trail. Just beyond the "Sentinel" pines adjacent to the North Star Run, the Trolls Bridge Run veers off toward the west and climbs a big hill before crossing the Trolls Bridge. It climbs another big hill before joining the Coxey Pond Trail and South Road junction. Intermediate skiers should be able to handle the uphill climbs when traveling from east to west. But the fast downhill run from west to east is more difficult and recommended for advanced skiers. Use caution on this difficult trail!

The **SOUTH ROAD** (.7 mile) intersects the junction of the Trolls Bridge Run and the Coxey Pond Trail. It provides a rather steep route back to the North Arm Road, with one difficult downhill section that is recommended for more experienced skiers.

FOR MORE INFORMATION: Contact the Kawishiwi Ranger District, United States Forest Service, 118 S. 4th Avenue East, Ely, MN 55731. Or call Camp Northland (218-365-2118) for lodging information and current snow conditions.

ST. PAUL YMCA CAMPS

DIRECTOR: Randy Fulton
ADDRESS: 1761 University Avenue West, St. Paul, MN 55104
PHONE: (612) 645-2136
LODGING: Housekeeping cabins at Camp DuNord; sleeping units at Camp Northland. Accommodations for 2 to 30 people.
DINING: Meals are served family-style in the Dining Hall for Camp Northland guests, by reservation only.
AMENITIES: Saunas at both camps; central shower building at Camp Northland.
COMMENTS: Camp DuNord and Camp Northland are neighboring resort facilities on the lovely North Arm of Burntside Lake, adjacent to the North Arm Trails system. Both camps are owned and operated by the St. Paul YMCA, but managed as separate facilities with somewhat distinct "personalities."

Camp DuNord was one of the pioneers in the Ely area cross country skiing business. Its rustic accommodations have long served as retreats for Twin Cities residents. And, in cooperation with the U.S. Forest Service, it is largely responsible for developing the fine system of ski trails along the North Arm. Cabins there range from a one-room accommodation that sleeps two, to Thor's Lodge, a 4-bedroom facility with a large loft that sleeps 30. Most of the cabins have fireplaces and/or lake views. All are equipped for housekeeping, but none has running water. Outdoor biffies are located near the cabins. There are no shower facilities, but a nice sauna is available to all guests. Guests are responsible for supplying their own bedding.

Camp Northland is a newcomer to winter tourism. Its newly refurbished cabins accommodate from 3 to 12 people. Although running water is also not available here, there is a central shower facility, as well as a sauna. Meals are served family-style in the attractive dining room.

Camp DuNord offers housekeeping cabins on the shore of beautiful Burntside Lake.

A large fireplace warms skiers in the dining room at Camp Northland.

The Hegman Lakes Trail

Use Level: Moderate

Trail Type: Natural environment, not machine goomed and track-set

Difficulty: Intermediate

Trail Length: 4-8 miles

Maps: Available at Kawishiwi District Ranger or Chamber of Commerce in Ely.

Highlights: Indian pictographs, long downhill run at beginning, old pines

Trailhead: South Hegman Lake is located ten miles (by air) due north of Ely. From the Chamber of Commerce cabin (junction of Highways 1 and 169), drive east on Highway 169 for one mile, to its intersection with County Road 88. Turn left there and follow this good road for 2.3 miles to the Echo Trail (County Road 116). Turn right and follow the Echo Trail for 11.4 miles to the Hegman Lake parking lot.

Description: Most people who use this trail are content to ski the two-mile course across South Hegman and North Hegman lakes to the excellent display of Indian rock paintings near Trease Lake, and then return via the same route — a round-trip distance of four miles. More adventurous (and more advanced) skiers may continue skiing north from the pictographs, across Trease Lake, and then follow the Trease Lake portage to the Angleworm Trail, which will lead them back to the Echo Trail — an 8-mile loop in all. Except for the Echo Trail, all of the route is contained within the BWCA Wilderness.

Indian pictographs on North Hegman Lake.

163

The Hegman Lakes Trail passes through a narrow channel between Trease Lake and North Hegman Lake.

From the east side of the parking lot, this route first follows a ¼-mile downhill portage trail to South Hegman Lake. It is usually well-packed by previous skiers. When there is insufficient snow on the ground, however, protruding rocks may present a hazard. Be alert! Most of the trail slopes down gradually, but there are three steep (though short) drops that may be difficult for inexperienced skiers. The final precipitous plunge, in fact, is over a log stairway down to the lake. If you prefer to walk down this steep slope, please stay off to the side of the trail, to avoid making the trail any worse than it already is for those who dare to ski over it.

Unless you have arrived immediately after a snowfall, it is likely that the portage trail will be packed. Because of its occasional steepness, which may necessitate the use of herringbone steps or parallel side steps by those returning (uphill), don't expect a good set of tracks. On your uphill return trip, you will have more time to view the towering pines that thrive along the trail. They are nearly 150 years old.

Near the base of the trail is a junction with another trail that leads to North Hegman Lake. This alternate route to the pictographs is more difficult than the lake route, and it is not suitable for skiing unless there is plenty of snow on the ground. Most skiers employ the lake route.

From the base of the portage, turn left and ski along the west shore of South Hegman Lake to the short portage trail connecting South Hegman and North Hegman lakes. Be alert to open water near the portage (or weak ice) where a small creek enters South Hegman.

Continue your trek on North Hegman Lake, following the northwest shoreline to the north end of the lake. There, just before the creek leading to Trease Lake, is a rocky cliff containing some of the most discernible Indian rock paintings in the entire Boundary Waters Canoe Area Wilderness.

The origins of these, and many other, pictographs in this region are shrouded in mystery. No one knows for certain WHO painted them or WHY they were painted. But it is generally accepted that these fascinating symbols were created several hundred years ago and probably had great significance to the artists. Most notable among the reddish-brown figures that you may view are a moose and a wolf (or dog), two canoes, and a human-like creature that probably represents a Maymayguishi. The Maymayguishi was the Indian equivalent of the Irish leprechaun — a mischievous little creature that played tricks on the Indians, such as stealing their fish. In addition, there are some abstract tally marks painted on the rocks nearby. Take time to observe closely the pictographs, but please do not touch them. They represent the only written legacy of an ancient woodland culture that once thrived in this part of North America.

SIDE TRIP: For skiers who desire a longer trek, the 1½-mile journey to the northeast end of Little Bass Lake (3 miles round-trip) affords a very pleasant extension. In fact, any one of three campsites there is a good place to stop and cook your lunch. By then backtracking your route to the trailhead, you will have enjoyed a 7-mile ski through some of the loveliest landscape in the North Country.

For more advanced, and more ambitious, skiers, backtracking may be avoided by continuing to ski north from the pictographs to the Angleworm Trail and then looping back to the trailhead via the Echo Trail (or leaving a second car at the Angleworm parking lot). First ski across Trease Lake to its northwest shoreline, where you will find the beginning of a seldom-used portage trail. At this point, the well-tracked trail that you have been using will likely end. The Trease portage is much more difficult, passing over rolling terrain, and frequently barricaded by windfalls. The path, itself, is sometimes hard to discern. Use your compass, if necessary, to be certain that you are skiing in a northerly direction. Eventually, persistence will pay off, and you will find yourself at the junction of the Angleworm Trail.

Turn left, and follow the Angleworm Trail to the Echo Trail. Then ski or walk along the Echo Trail south (left) to the Hegman Lakes trailhead. (See The Angelworm Lake-Spring Creek Loop for details.)

FOR MORE INFORMATION: Contact the Kawishiwi District Ranger, United States Forest Service, 118 S. 4th Avenue East, Ely, MN 55731.

Melting snow results in ice "sculptures" on the cliffs of North Hegman Lake.

The Angleworm Lake — Spring Creek Loop

Use Level: Light

Trail Type: Natural environment, not machine groomed and track-set

Difficulty: Advanced

Trail Length: 16 miles

Maps: Available from the Kawishiwi District Ranger or the Chamber of Commerce in Ely.

Highlights: Beautiful wilderness lakes route, with challenging hills for experienced skiers.

Trailhead: 17 miles north of Ely. From the Chamber of Commerce Building in Ely, drive east on Highway 169 for one mile to its junction with County Road 88. Turn left and drive 2.3 miles to the Echo Trail. (County Road 116). Turn right and follow the Echo Trail for 13.2 miles to the Angleworm parking lot on the right side of the road.

Description: Skiers who are familiar with most of the Ely area trails usually rank this one among their favorites. It is one of the longest, and one of the most beautiful loops in the Ely area. It is primarily because of its length, in fact, that the trail is recommended for advanced skiers. Intermediate-level skiers could also enjoy the Angleworm Lake portage trail to the south end of Angleworm Lake. But only the most experienced skiers should consider tackling a 16-mile loop — especially one that penetrates so deeply into the roadless wilderness, where one's survival during adverse conditions might depend entirely on one's resourcefulness. Intermediate skiers, however, might consider either stretching this loop over a 2-day period or joining the bottom part of this loop with the Hegman Lakes Trail, 8 miles round trip (See The Hegman Lakes Trail).

As you might expect, the easiest parts of the Angleworm Loop are across the lakes. But at the same time, care should be exercised when crossing the lakes. Weak ice and slush are potential hazards on lake surfaces.

Although the trail is not groomed, it is usually skier-tracked into Angleworm Lake. Beyond the lake, itself, there may be no tracks, however. Your travel rate, therefore, may be much slower than when you are skiing on nicely groomed trails. Judge your time on the trail accordingly.

The trail begins on nearly level terrain, then gradually descends, and finally drops steeply down to cross Spring Creek. East of the creek, the trail is more difficult, climbing to a ridge and then passing over several small hills en route to an intersection with two other trails near the south end of Angleworm Lake. The trail leading south from this junction goes to Trease Lake and joins the Hegman Lakes Trail. The middle trail is for hikers heading for the east side of Angleworm Lake. It is not a good trail on which to ski. The northernmost trail is the best route to Angelworm Lake. Although the trail continues north along the west side of Anglworm Lake, it is not recommended for skiers. The only feasible route, therefore, is on the lake itself.

Angleworm is one of the prettiest lakes in the BWCA Wilderness. Its long, slender profile is bordered by steep pine-covered hills that create a winter wonderland for skiers. If mid-day is approaching when you reach the north end of the lake, you should probably consider backtracking to the trailhead. For skiers with plenty of time left, though, the route continues from the north end of Angleworm Lake down a 220-yard gentle slope to Home Lake.

At the north end of Home Lake, skiers have two choices. The shortest route follows beaver ponds from the northwest corner of Home Lake north to Beartrap Lake. But this is a difficult trail that will require "bushwhacking" along the way. The most frequently used route employs a chain of lakes and portages that loops toward the northeast. Remember that these trails were not designed for skiers. Sharp turns, steep grades and narrow paths may make skiing hazardous. The longest of the portage trails (¾ mile) connects the northeast end of Home Lake with the west side of Gull Lake. It climbs rather steeply to more than 80 feet above Home Lake. But then there is a long downhill run to Gull Lake that drops over 120 feet in all.

North of Gull Lake, the trail leads across a bog en route to Mudhole Lake. An overland trail connecting Mudhole and Thunder lakes surmounts a small hill that may result in a fast downhill run to Thunder Lake. After crossing Thunder and Beartrap lakes, the route drops gently down a portage trail for 5/8 mile to the Beartrap River, which, in turn, leads a short distance west to its junction with Spring Creek.

Upon reaching Spring Creek, the trail turns south and follows an old road along the west side of the marsh bordering the creek. This is better than skiing on the creek, itself, because the road doesn't wind nearly as much as the creek. Spring Creek draw is quite scenic, bordered by a steep ridge on the west that looms more than 200 feet above the creek.

This route follows Spring Creek south to the point where it is crossed by the Angleworm Trail. The parking lot and trailhead is about a mile southwest of this junction.

FOR MORE INFORMATION: Contact the Kawishiwi District Ranger, United States Forest Service, 118 S. 4th Avenue East, Ely, MN 55731.

A log bridge crosses Spring Creek, near the midpoint of the Angleworm portage trail.

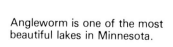

Angleworm is one of the most beautiful lakes in Minnesota.

Stuart River-
Baldpate Lake Trails

Use Level: Light

Trail Type: Natural environment, not machine groomed and track-set

Difficulty: Intermediate and beginner

Trail Length: 10 miles. Loops ranging from 2¼ miles (Beginner) to 6 miles (Intermediate)

Maps: Available from the Kawishiwi District Ranger or the Chamber of Commerce in Ely.

Highlights: Sentinel pine, moose area, interesting variety of woodland habitats.

Trailhead: This ski area is located about fifteen miles (by air) northwest of Ely, adjacent to the Echo Trail. From the Chamber of Commerce building, drive east on Highway 169 for one mile. Turn left on County Road 88 and drive 2.3 miles to its junction with County Road 116, the Echo Trail. Turn right there, and follow the winding Echo Trail for 17.3 miles to the Stuart River parking lot on the right side of the road, nearly a mile past the entrance to Lodge of the Whispering Pines.

Description: These trails offer a good opportunity for a near-wilderness setting that should accommodate nearly all levels of skiing through a series of interconnecting loops. Since they receive only light use, the trails are likely to NOT be tracked and are seldom groomed. They pass through one of the best areas to view moose, and through an interesting variety of tree species, with impressive stands of jack pine, red pine and black spruce, as the trail varies from ridge top to valleys of bog. The trails are marked with blue diamonds only at intersections. Carry a compass!

Skiers are confronted with a choice of several possible loops, ranging in distance from the 2-mile loop through a spruce bog to a 6-mile loop that follows the perimeter of the whole area. In addition, during the mid-winter deep-freeze, you may wish to extend your skiing experience on either Big Lake or the Stuart River. But, if you do this, always be alert to hazardous ice conditions.

After a long, frozen winter, the Stuart River begins to flow again in March.

STUART RIVER PORTAGE TRAIL (1.6 miles): As the name implies, this trail serves canoeists during the summer. It begins at the north end of the parking lot and follows a predominantly downhill course most of the way to the river. You'll see six canoe rests along the trail. To the third rest, the terrain is mostly rolling. After the third rest, the trail slopes more steeply. But the steepest hill is just after the fourth rest, just beyond the sign designating the border of the Boundary Waters Canoe Area Wilderness. Approach this steep downhill slope with caution (when traveling north), since there may be windfalls across the path. At the fifth canoe rest, a blue diamond marks the beginning of the Pine Meadows Trail on the right (east) side of the portage trail. The Stuart River is less than a half mile north of this junction. From there, when the ice is safe, you may ski along the Stuart River in either direction. If you follow the river upstream (to the east), however, you will encounter several small rapids around which you may have to "bushwhack" and carry your skis. On the other hand, when you follow the river downstream (toward Stuart Lake), you may employ portage paths to circumnavigate the occasional rapids.

Jackpine is the dominate tree species along this trail, but there are also several nice stands of Norway pine, dating up to 200 years old. About a half mile from the Echo Trail, you will ski past a mammoth white pine that is from 300 to 350 years old. It's hard to conceive that this sentinel pine was an impressive size when the United States was born! The stories it could tell . . .

PINE MEADOWS TRAIL (2 miles): This trail connects the Stuart River Portage Trail with Baldpate Lake and the other two trails south of the lake. It passes through thick stands of jackpine and spruce and crosses open marsh meadows.

RIDGE TRAIL (1¼ miles): This trail follows an old logging road between Baldpate Lake and the Echo Trail at a point .8 mile southeast of the parking area, merely .1 mile northwest of the entrance to Lodge of the Whispering Pines. You'll be skiing through second-growth jackpine and red pine. Moose frequent the area.

SPRUCE BOG TRAILS (3½ miles total): There are two access points for these trails. One trail begins at the Echo Trail, just .1 mile southeast of the entrance to Lodge of the Whispering Pines. Another trail begins .4 mile beyond the resort (toward Ely). Both offer easy loops across swamps that follow old winter logging roads. They offer beginners an opportunity to experience the essence of wilderness amidst the thick growth of black spruce. The Spruce Bog Trail will also lead the more ambitious skier to Baldpate Lake, where the Pine Meadows and Ridge trails meet.

A RECOMMENDED ROUTE (6 miles): From the parking lot at the Stuart River Portage, first head south, cross the Echo Trail and ski downhill to Big Lake via the Big Lake portage trail. Follow the north shoreline of Big Lake east to Lodge of Whispering Pines. A trail connects from there to the Spruce Bog Trail. Follow it to Baldpate Lake and then join the Pine Meadows Trail. When you reach the Stuart River Portage, turn left and ski uphill to the parking lot. This enjoyable loop will give you a taste of nearly all that the wilderness has to offer.

FOR MORE INFORMATION: Contact the Kawishiwi District Ranger, United States Forest Service, 118 S. 4th Avenue East, Ely, MN 55731.

Stuart Lake Trail

Use Level: Light

Trail Type: Natural Environment, not machine groomed and track-set

Difficulty: Intermediate

Trail Length: 16 miles round-trip

Maps: Available from the La Croix Ranger District.

Highlights: Wide trail that penetrates deep within the Boundary Waters Wilderness

Trailhead: Off the Echo Trail (County Road 116), approximately 1½ miles east of the eastern end of Forest Road 464. This is about 22 miles northwest of County Road 88 (26 miles from Ely) and 27 miles east of County Road 24 at Buyck.

Description: The Stuart Lake Trail is a wilderness route that receives little use and is not likely to be tracked. Recommended for experienced skiers, the 16-mile round trip is probably too much to accomplish in just one day. For campers, there is a nice campsite at the trail's end on Stuart Lake; and from there, there are several possible side trips to extend one's winter outing. For an interesting change of pace, it may also be possible to return to the Echo Trail via the Stuart River canoe route. This would require skiing on the frozen river and utilizing several short portage trails around fast-water stretches. Of course, caution must be employed while skiing on the river.

Formerly called the La Croix Trail, the Stuart Lake Trail was once an administrative trail leading to a Forest Service cabin on Lac La Croix. The trail was abandonned and not maintained for many years, until the Youth Conservation Corps restored it to Stuart Lake. Now the trail is wide and rather smooth, with several good, gentle downhill runs.

The trail begins in an open meadow and initially heads northwest from the trailhead parking area north of the Echo Trail. It then veers north to closely skirt the west side of a 200-foot hill and the west shore of Mule Lake, and finally angles northeast to the east shore of Stuart Lake. All but the first ¼ mile lies in the Boundary Waters Canoe Area Wilderness. Although federal regulations pertaining to travel permits and campsite locations are not in effect during the winter months, all other regulations do apply, including the prohibition of cans and bottles. Skiers should be aware of, and obey, any and all of the wilderness regulations.

Much of the trail crosses rolling terrain through a mixture of forest habitat. Near the south end of Stuart Lake, the trail crosses the Stuart River at a rapids. The trail then intersects two portage trails as it follows along the east side of Stuart Lake to the trail's end at a campsite on the northeast shore of the lake. About ¼ mile beyond the first intersection with a portage trail, you may want to leave the main trail to visit a scenic overlook. At a clearing in the woods, one may ski west through sparsely wooded terrain to a bald ridge that sits more than 130 feet above Stuart Lake. From that point, one may enjoy a lovely panorama of the lake and the surrounding countryside.

Winter campers looking for an extended trek may ski northeast from Stuart Lake to Iron Lake on the Canadian border, following portage trails to several small lakes en route. Curtain Falls, which cascades into Iron Lake at its east end, is gorgeous at any time of year! But be extremely cautious of weak ice and open water as you approach the bottom of the rapids below the falls.

FOR MORE INFORMATION: Contact either the La Croix District Ranger, Box 1085, Cook, MN 55723, or the Kawishiwi District Ranger, 118 S. 4th Avenue East, Ely, MN 55731.

The Fernberg Tower Trail winds through a delightful variety of Northwoods terrain.

Big Moose Trail

Use Level: Light

Trail Type: Natural environment, not machine groomed and track-set

Difficulty: Intermediate

Trail Length: 4 miles (round-trip)

Maps: Available from the La Croix District Ranger.

Highlights: Nice stands of jackpine and red pine

Trailhead: Adjacent to Forest Road 464, 1½ miles south of its junction with County Road 116 (Echo Trail). This is about 30 miles northwest of Ely, and about 27 miles east of Buyck.

Description: This 2-mile route leads south from Forest Road 464, crosses several hills that enable some short downhill runs, and ends at the northern tip of Big Moose Lake. Most of the rolling landscape is covered with red pine and jackpine, and the trail is wide and smooth much of the way. The roughest part of the trail is near the beginning. When Forest Road 464 is not plowed, skiers must park at the junction of F.R. 464 and the Echo Trail — 1½ miles north of the trailhead.

Within a half mile of the trailhead, the trail crosses two old winter roads. Bear slightly left as you cross the roads, and watch for snow-capped rock cairns that mark the way. Near the south end of the trail, as you ski past a pond, you'll enter the Boundary Waters Canoe Area Wilderness. Although a travel permit is not required during the winter, other BWCAW regulations do apply to those venturing all the way to Big Moose Lake.

Experienced skiers might use this as a starting trail for an extended loop east to Big Lake and back to the Echo Trail and the Stuart River Trail parking lot. This requires a good deal of lake skiing, and two long portage trails connect Big Moose, Duck and Big lakes. Of course, cars would have to be shuttled between the two trailheads.

FOR MORE INFORMATION: Contact either the La Croix District Ranger, Box 1085, Cook, MN 55723, or the Kawishiwi District Ranger, 118 S. 4th Avenue East, Ely, MN 55731.

Norway Trail

Use Level: Light

Trail Type: Natural environment, not machine groomed and track-set

Difficulty: Intermediate

Trail Length: 16 miles (round-trip)

Maps: Available from the La Croix District Ranger in Cook.

Highlights: Stand of magnificent old Norway pines

Trailhead: One mile south of the Echo Trail (County Road 116), ¼ mile east of the Lake Jeanette Campground. From the Chamber of Commerce building in Ely, it is a drive of almost 40 miles up the Echo

Trail to the Nigh Creek Road (Forest Route 471). Turn left and follow this road for one mile to the trailhead and small parking area. This is about 23 miles east of Buyck. If there is too much snow on the Nigh Creek Road, you'll have to park along the Echo Trail and ski to the trailhead.

Description: The Norway Trail follows an old fire tower access route from the old Echo Trail south to Trout Lake. The last half mile of the trail adjoining Trout Lake falls within the Boundary Waters Canoe Area Wilderness. Although no permit is required during the winter months, all other BWCAW regulations do apply to users who venture this far south. Since the trail is not groomed and often not even tracked by previous skiers, it allows skiers to experience a sense of wilderness exploration through an interesting mixture of forest habitats on rolling terrain that is challenging to intermediate-level skiers. Because of its length, however, only experienced skiers, who are well aware of their own limitations and the possible hazards, should even consider skiing the entire trail in one day. For most ski-campers, the trail would make a good 2-day winter camping route.

Since the trail crosses a logging road that connects to the Nigh Creek Road, a nice 7-mile loop is available for skiers who prefer to tackle only a portion of the Norway Trail. Like the trail itself, the roads cross over a number of hills that enable some fast downhill runs.

The Nigh Creek Road is not likely to be plowed. When the snow depth is too great to permit driving to the trailhead, therefore, the ski trek must begin at the Echo Trail. The trail then begins at an old gravel pit and follows the original Echo Trail for ¼ mile. After crossing Nigh Creek, the Norway Trail veers south from the old road and follows the creek. Soon it leaves the creek and passes over rolling terrain that is covered with a mixture of timber.

Upon reaching the logging spur road, skiers have the option of looping west on it to the Nigh Creek Road and skiing 3½ miles back to the trailhead. Or they may continue southbound, cross Norway Creek and climb a sidehill to an area that is cluttered with spruce and jackpine windfalls. It may be difficult to see the trail there, so watch carefully for timber that was sawn to clear the path.

Beyond the blowdown area is the highlight of the route — a magnificent stand of old Norway (red) pine trees. At one time there was a ranger cabin here and a fire look-out tower nearby. From there the trail continues south and crosses a beaver drainage en route to the North Arm of Trout Lake.

It's a strenuous 8-mile trek to Trout Lake. At least on the return trip, you'll have tracks to follow!

FOR MORE INFORMATION: Contact either the La Croix District Ranger, Box 1085, Cook, MN 55723, or the Kawishiwi District Ranger, 118 S. 4th Avenue East, Ely, MN 55731.

Sioux-Hustler Trail

Use Level: Light

Trail Type: Natural environment, not machine groomed and track-set

Difficulty: Advanced

Trail Length: 28 miles

Maps: Available from the La Croix District Ranger in Cook or the Kawishiwi District Ranger in Ely.

Highlights: Devil's Cascade; remote wilderness isolation; moose habitat

Trailhead: At the Meander Lake Picnic Grounds, on Forest Route 467 (Meander Lake Road), 22 miles east of County Road 23 (approximately 29 miles northwest of Ely). The trailhead is signed and has space for vehicle parking. Neither the parking area nor the Meander Lake Road, however, may be plowed. Consequently, parking may have to be along the Echo Trail. Another option is to park at the Little Indian Sioux River and ski north on the river to Elm Portage, where the Sioux-Hustler Trail intersects the river.

Even in mid-winter, there is open water on the Little Indian Sioux River at Elm Portage.

Description: The Sioux-Hustler Trail is one of the longest and one of the most challenging loops in the Arrowhead region. 22 of its 28 miles lie within the Boundary Waters Wilderness. Although both ends of the loop occasionally receive winter visitors, the isolated interior part of the trail is seldom seen by skiers. The trail was designed for hikers, not skiers. It's not as wide as most ski trails, and downhill runs may have sharp turns that are difficult to negotiate. In open areas, it may even be difficult to find the trail. Few skiers could complete the entire loop in just one day. Indeed, under such rugged skiing conditions, most skiers would need at least two and possible three days to complete the course. The Forest Service recommends that only the very experienced ski-camper should venture further than a day's trek on the Sioux-Hustler Trail. Less experienced skiers, however, might enjoy the 5-mile trek to Devil's Cascade (one way) at the west end of the loop, or the 7-mile journey (one way) to Emerald Lake at the east end of the loop.

From the trailhead at Meander Lake, the trail first angles off toward the northwest to skirt the east edge of the Little Indian Sioux River. The terrain varies considerably from ridge tops to marsh-rimmed creeks, providing several fast downhill runs along the way. At Elm Portage along the Sioux River, this trail joins a trail that originates 7 miles west of Meander Lake. The route then continues along the east shore of the river for about a mile. South of Lower Pauness Lake, the trail veers toward the northeast and climbs to a ridge more than 180 feet above the lake. After a good, long downhill run, the trail again climbs to a high ridge overlooking scenic Devil's Cascade, where the Little Indian Sioux River plunges 75 feet through a steep granite gorge bordered by hills towering more than 200 feet above the water. The panoramic view from the overlook above the cascade is well worth the effort it takes to ski there. For most skiers, this is a great place to stop, rest, eat lunch and then backtrack to the trailhead.

Skiers continuing around the loop will follow a ridgeline above the Sioux River and then drop down to beaver flowages where beaver dams are used as part of the trail. The south shore of Pageant Lake marks the northernmost point of the Sioux-Hustler loop. A campsite on the south shore of the lake is accessible from the trail. From Pageant Lake, the trail heads southeast and winds past the east shore of Range Line Lake, two miles south of Pageant Lake.

From Range Line Lake to Emerald Lake the trail climbs to a ridgetop, intersects the Oyster-Hustler portage, and continues on past the junction of a spur trail which leads to the campsite on Emerald Lake. South of Emerald Lake, skiers pass through a 15,000-acre region that burned in 1971. Across two beaver flowages and through tall marsh grasses, the trail is sometimes difficult to see. About one mile south of Meander Lake, the trail climbs 150 feet from a low marshland to an overlook that affords skiers an excellent view of the massive region that was burned by the Little Indian Sioux Fire.

Throughout this rugged loop, the terrain is quite hilly and the trail is likely to be blocked on frequent occasions with windfalls. An interesting variety of ridgetops, creek valleys and beaver ponds leaves little opportunity for skiers to be bored on this long route. The biggest problem is probably the tendency to bite off more than one can chew. Know your limitations!

Another access to the Sioux-Hustler Trail begins at the Echo Trail 1.1 miles west of the Little Indian Sioux River. It is more likely to be skier-tracked than the main trailhead at the Meander Lake Picnic Grounds. Skiers may enjoy a pleasant round-trip journey by starting there, skiing on the down-sloping course to Elm Portage, and then following the Sioux River back to the Echo Trail, one mile from the origin. A side-trip to Devil's Cascade will double the amount of time required. The whole route is likely to be skier tracked, if more than a couple weeks have elapsed since the most recent snowfall.

FOR MORE INFORMATION: Contact either the La Croix District Ranger, Box 1085, Cook, MN 55723, or the Kawishiwi District Ranger, 118 S. 4th Avenue East, Ely, MN 55731.

The Sioux-Hustler Trail is one of the longest and most challenging loops in the Arrowhead.

Astrid Lake Trails

Use Level: Light

Trail Type: Natural environment, not machine groomed and track-set

Difficulty: Beginner and Intermediate

Trail Length: 7 miles (1-way, with 2 optional loops)

Maps: Available from the La Croix District Ranger, United States Forest Service.

Highlights: Good blend of lakes and forest habitats

Trailhead: Jeanette Lake Campground, adjacent to County Road 116. From the junction of the Echo Trail and County Road 24, nine miles south of Crane Lake, drive east for 11.9 miles. Or from Ely, drive on the Echo Trail for 34 miles from County Road 88 (37.3 miles from Ely). Turn north on Forest Road 360 toward the campground. A small parking area is on the right side of the road, .1 mile north of the Echo Trail.

Description: The Astrid Lake trail system connects Jeanette, Nigh, Astrid and Maude lakes. Skiers have the option of skiing on frozen lake surfaces and the interconnecting overland trails, or skiing entirely on the 7 miles of hiking trails that loop around the lakes. Most of the rolling landscape is covered with dense stands of jackpine and a delightful smattering of enormous red and white pine trees. Sparsely forested ridge tops and secluded valleys filled with frozen beaver ponds add to the variety.

Trail intersections are not signed, except at the canoe portages, so it is important that skiers carry maps and compasses. Blue ribbons attached to trees and shrubs help to mark the way. Rock cairns are also used on the main "corridor trail."

The Astrid-Maude portages intersect Forest Road 200 near the west end of the trail system. This alternate starting point is 2½ miles south of the Echo Trail, 6¼ miles from the trailhead at Lake Jeanette.

The whole system consists of 1.3 miles of excellent canoe portage trails and 5.7 miles of less improved hiking trails. The **JEANETTE-to-MAUDE LAKES TRAIL** (4.3 miles 1 way) starts at the Lake Jeanette trailhead and, serves as the main corridor trail to the west end at Maude Lake. The beginning of the route is quite level, with only one small hill separating Lake Jeanette from the northeast shore of Nigh Lake. The trail then skirts the west edge of a large swamp, and then begins the gradual ascent of a high ridge that towers 140 feet above the swamp. At the summit of the ridge is the junction of the Astrid Lake Loop, which leads off toward the west. The main trail to Maude Lake continues in a southbound direction along the top of the ridge.

At 2.2 miles from the trailhead, the trail drops down off the ridge, crosses a small creek, and skirts the south edge of a large beaver pond. Southwest of the pond, the trail winds across a rolling landscape that is forested with a blend of mature jackpine, paper birch and aspen.

Just east of Astrid Lake, there is a junction with the south end of the Astrid Lake Loop. Bearing left at that point, the trail to Maude Lake continues toward the southwest and descends the valley of Crellin Creek.

After crossing Crellin Creek, the level trail skirts the south end of Astrid Lake and then joins the 1/4-mile uphill portage trail from Astrid Lake to Forest Road 200. Beyond the road, the trail slopes gently down to the east shore of Maude Lake.

The **ASTRID LAKE LOOP** (1.6 miles 1-way) offers skiers a more challenging route to the east shore of Astrid Lake. It loops west from the main corridor trail and affords skiers a panoramic overlook toward Lake Jeanette and the vast Superior National Forest. After crossing several small hills, the trail begins a long, gradual descent through a dense forest of mature jackpines. At its first junction with the Nigh-Pauline Lakes Loop near the base of the long hill, the Astrid Lake Loop veers left and surmounts a small hill en route to its second junction with the Nigh-Pauline Loop. Leading southward, the trail passes several huge red and white pines and soon skirts the northeast shore of Astrid Lake. At its second junction with the Jeanette-to-Maude Lake Trail, skiers may loop back toward the northeast and return to the trailhead for a trek totalling 6.3 miles. Or continue westbound on the trail to Maude Lake.

The **NIGH-PAULINE LAKES LOOP** (1.1 mile) is an extension of the Astrid Lake Loop. The level to gently sloping terrain should pose no threat to inexperienced skiers. At the north end of the loop, the trail joins the Nigh-Pauline portage. At that point, skiers may either head northeast across Nigh Lake to rejoin the main trail from Lake Jeanette (a total loop of about 4½ miles) or ski southwest to join the Astrid Lake Loop again.

FOR MORE INFORMATION: Contact the La Croix District Ranger, Box 1085, Cook, MN 55723.

CHAPTER 9

VOYAGEUR COUNTRY

Voyageur Country occupies the northwesternmost part of the Arrowhead. Voyageurs National Park, Kabetogama State Forest and the northwestern tip of Superior National Forest provide skiers with thousands of acres of government lands that are available for cross country exploration. But, currently, there are only a few scattered ski-designated trails in the region. Most are lightly used. Consequently, this area is a great place for skiers to get away from it all.

Plans are currently underway to develop an extensive network of groomed trails around the west end of Lake Vermilion. Most of the 39-mile Ashawa Ski Trail should be completed by the winter of 1986-87. When completed, it will nearly double the designated trail mileage in Voyageur Country.

Small popluation centers are also scattered across the region. The tiny towns of Cook, Crane Lake, Orr and Ray are most closely situated to the ski trails included in this guide. Gasoline, groceries and food service are available to resort guests in all of these towns, as well as in other area villages. Cross country skis and equipment are available for rent at Dill's Sportsmen's Service in Crane Lake. Skiers who are not lodging in the area should be aware that food and automotive services may not be readily available in the immediate vicinities of the ski trailheads.

As new trails are constructed in the area, more resorts will be winterizing their facilities. For the latest developments, and for more information about the towns and resort associations in Voyageur Country, contact the following organizations:

Crane Lake Commercial Club
Crane Lake, MN 55725

Kabetogama Lake Association
Ray, MN 56669

Lake Vermilion Resort Association
Cook, MN 55723

Pelican Lake — Orr Resort Association
Box MA
Orr, MN 55771

Ash River Trail Commercial Club
Box A82
Ash River Trail, Orr, MN 55771

The Herriman Lake Trail leads to a breathtaking overlook across the Echo River valley.

A good wooden bridge permits safe crossings of the Echo River, en route to the Herriman Lake Trails.

Herriman Lake Trails

Use Level: Light

Trail Type: Natural environment, usually not machine groomed and track-set

Difficulty: Intermediate

Trail Length: 14½ miles

Maps: Available from the La Croix District Ranger.

Highlights: Varied terrain, including some panoramic vistas

Trailhead: About 2 miles southeast of Crane Lake. From Buyck, drive north on County Road 24 for almost 10 miles to the junction of County Road 424. Turn right and drive another 2 miles east and north to the signed trailhead on the east side of the road. Parking is available on the west side of the road.

Description: This is a scenic network of trails that winds throughout a 10-square mile region between the Echo River on the west and the Canadian border on the east. In between are numerous hills that will challenge intermediate skiers and open ridges that will delight anyone with the scenic views they permit. Loops of different lengths enable skiers to enjoy a pleasant half-day outing or an all-day trek into the Boundary Waters Canoe Area Wilderness. The snowmobile club at Crane Lake has USFS authorization to groom these trails when requested to do so.

More than half of the trails lie within the BWCAW. Although travel permits are not required of skiers, all other wilderness regulations are in effect. No trail signs are used in the wilderness, and only a minimum of signing is used elsewhere. For winter campers, there are three BWCAW campsites along the trail system, accessible by spur trails off the main routes.

The trail begins on the east side of County Road 424, across from the parking lot, and extends east for .4 mile to a picnic site along the Echo River. A bridge there permits a safe crossing over the rapids. Just beyond the bridge is a trail intersection. The **LITTLE VERMILION LAKE TRAIL** continues eastward, past the north end of Knute Lake and on to the southwest shore of Little Vermilion Lake, about 3.2 miles from the trailhead.

Just east of Knute Lake, the **KNUTE LAKE LOOP** (1.8 miles) intersects the trail to Little Vermilion Lake. It leads south and climbs along the side of a big hill, which affords a long downhill run that drops more than 120 feet to an intersection with the Herriman Lake Trail. It then loops back toward the northeast and rejoins the Little Vermilion Lake Trail about a mile east of Knute Lake.

From the bottom of the Knute Lake Loop, the **HERRIMAN LAKE TRAIL** (1.8 miles) switches back to skirt the south side of Herriman Lake and intersect the Echo River Trail. This is the most difficult trail in the system. There is a scenic overlook above the south shore of Herriman Lake.

The **ECHO RIVER TRAIL** (3.7 miles) begins just east of the picnic site and leads southeast for about three miles to a bald ridgetop south of

Baylis Lake. It is the easiest of the Herriman Lake Trails, following the gently rolling landscape that borders the Echo River. Near the south end however, the trail climbs more than 150 feet to an alpine-looking ridge that affords excellent vistas of the Echo River valley and the vast Superior National Forest. The trail circles around the top of the ridge and then rejoins itself.

At the other end of the system, the **DOVRE LAKE LOOP** swings north from the Little Vermilion Lake Trail about ⅓ mile east of the picnic site. Along the 4-mile course of this trail, it crosses a number of ledgerock outcroppings and provides good views of Dovre Lake, beaver ponds and the surrounding forest. It rejoins the Little Vermilion Lake Trail at an intersection just north of Knute Lake.

FOR MORE INFORMATION: Contact the La Croix District Ranger, United States Forest Service, Box 1085, Cook, MN 55723.

Voyageurs National Park

Voyageurs National Park provides skiers with 219,000 acres of federally preserved lakes and forests along the Canadian border between International Falls and Crane Lake. Included in that vast territory are more than 100 square miles of frozen lakes dotted with hundreds of islands in a Northwoods setting that is truly awesome. Established only ten years ago, Voyageurs is the newest of the national parks and still a secret to most Americans and even to many Minnesotans.

During the summer months, this is a park for boaters. During the long winter season, it offers virtually unlimited opportunities for skiers, snowshoers and snowmobilers to explore a lovely wilderness that few others see after Labor Day. Road access to the park is available at Crane Lake, from Highway 53 east of Ray, or from Highway 11 east of International Falls. This guide includes information about lodging available in St. Louis County. For additional information about lodging and amenities in the International Falls area, contact:

Greater International Falls Chamber of Commerce
Box 169A
International Falls, MN 56649

There is only one designated cross-country ski trail in Voyageurs National Park, located near the west end of the park. At one time, there was another trail near Crane Lake, but it was abandoned due to lack of use.

Black Bay Ski Trail

Use Level: Light to moderate

Trail Type: Groomed annually, not machine tracked

Difficulty: Mostly for beginners and intermediates

Trail Length: 8.6 miles

Maps: Available at Park Headquarters in International Falls

Highlights: Naturalist guided activities

Trailhead: From the east end of Highway 11, 12 miles east of International Falls, ice roads lead to trailheads at either end of the system, ½ mile to the Black Bay access, or 4 miles to Dove Bay.

Description: The Black Bay Ski Trail is composed of a series of loops that afford the opportunity to plan a tour according to the skill of the group. A 2¼-mile loop and a .9-mile loop are available for beginners and others who prefer level to mildly graded terrain. A 2.4-mile trail segment offers a challenging run over hilly landscape for advanced skiers. The remainder of the course is ideally suited for intermediates.

Deer, ruffed grouse, chickadees and other birds are often seen by skiers. Moose also roam the area, and a pack of six wolves is known to exist in this area. Over 30 wolves roam throughout the entire park. Wolf tracks and scat are often seen along the trail.

The forest habitat is a blend of aspen, birch, spruce, balsam fir and red and white pine. Cedar trees provide the favorite food for white-tailed deer.

Guided tours, including several moonlight ski tours, are offered by the Park staff on several occasions during the winter. For a schedule of upcoming events, and

FOR MORE INFORMATION: contact the Superintendent, Voyageurs National Park, Box 50, International Falls, MN 56649.

A warming hut sits at the mid-point of the Ash River "A" loop.

184

The Ash River Trail provides an excellent loop for novice skiers along the banks of the Ash River.

Ash River Falls Trail

Use Level: Light to Moderate

Trail Type: Machine groomed and track-set

Difficulty: Mostly beginner and intermediate, some advanced

Trail Length: 12.4 miles

Maps: Available from the Area Forest Supervisor in Orr, MN 55771.

Highlights: Nice woodland scenery and excellent tracked trails

Trailhead: Adjacent to the Ash River Trail (County Road 765), five miles east of Highway 53. The junction of County 765 and U.S. 53 is 26 miles north of Orr, and 29 miles south of International Falls. There is a small parking area at the trailhead, 100 yards north of County Road 765. A second trailhead and parking area is located one mile beyond (east of) the first.

Description: Located entirely within Kabetogama State Forest, just south of Voyageurs National Park, the Ash River Falls Trail is administered by the Minnesota Department of Natural Resources exclusively for hikers and cross country skiers. No motorized vehicles are permitted on the trail. Skiers must have state Ski Touring Licenses.

From the first trailhead and parking lot on the north side of County Road 765, the trail loops toward the south and crosses the road at a sharp bend ¼ mile east of the trailhead turn-off. Be alert to vehicles on the road as you ski across it. On the south side of the road, then, the trail system splits into two main loops. Loop "A" offers a fairly easy trail that winds through a variety of forest habitats en route to the Ash River. Most of the 5½-mile loop is rated for beginners, but there are a couple of more difficult stretches, with some swift downhill runs. A warming hut is located near the Ash River, at the farthest point from the trailhead.

Loop "B" provides a more challenging trail for more experienced skiers. The 6.8-mile trail first follows the easy path of a winter road. In the easternmost part of the trail network, however, the trail follows ridgelines and ravines where one may enjoy some spectacular scenery. After leaving the easy winter road, most of the trail sections are rated for intermediate skiers. At the eastern end of the system is the most difficult trail. Experienced skiers who prefer to head straight for the more challenging trails may want to begin at the second trailhead.

These trails receive light to moderate use on weekends and are nicely groomed by the D.N.R. There is abundant evidence of wildlife in the area, including many tracks of deer and wolves. Watch for signs as you ski quietly through this fine network of trails.

FOR MORE INFORMATION: Contact the Area Forest Supervisor, Department of Natural Resources, Orr, MN 55771. Or call (218) 757-3274 for current snow conditions.

Ashawa Ski Trail

Trail Length: 39 miles

Status: Under construction

Description: Plans have been prepared, financing has been approved, and construction has begun. When this guide went to press, however, the Ashawa Ski Trail was barely more than a dream in the minds of a few far-sighted promoters who formed the Ashawa Ski Club. Construction began in the fall of 1985. If all goes well, the longest ski trail network in Voyageur Country could be complete by the winter of 1986-87.

Plans call for the trail to form a "corridor trail" around the western part of Lake Vermilion, stretching up to Elbow Lake, with spur trails leading to several resorts along the route. Currently, Elbow Lake Lodge is the only resort with winterized accommodations along the route. When the trail system is completed and skiers begin to use it, however, five more resorts will make plans to offer winterized accommodations.

It's an ambitious project. When completed, the Ashawa Ski Trail may be the longest trail system in the Arrowhead west of Cook County.

FOR MORE INFORMATION: Contact Ray Ranta, Elbow Lake Lodge, P.O. Box 136, Cook, MN 55723.

Parts of the 39-mile Ashawa Ski Trail are ready for skiers.

The Crane Lake Neighborhood Trails

Use Level: Light

Trail Type: Machine groomed

Difficulty: Beginner

Trail Length: 5 miles

Connects to: Crane Lake Tower Ski Trail

Maps: Available at local resorts

Highlights: Vermilion River gorge; Interesting variety of forest habitats; many short loops available

Trailhead: At Bowser's Resort, Voyaguaire Houseboats or Anderson's Outfitters in Crane Lake

Description: The Crane Lake Neighborhood Trails are made up of three primary trails, groomed and tracked by the local snowmobile club, and numerous secondary trails that link up the main arteries. In addition, there are snowmobile trails, unplowed roads and the frozen surfaces of creeks and lakes that add scenic miles to the whole network of potential ski routes in the Crane Lake neighborhood.

The **GORGE TRAIL** (1 mile one-way) begins at Voyaguaire Houseboats and extends west to "the gorge," a spectacular narrow canyon through which the Vermilion River is squeezed. The trail climbs a gradual hill at the beginning and then levels off for the remainder of the first half-mile. The last half of the trail then drops over 200 feet en route to the river's edge. The route follows the good path of an old logging road. Be cautious near the river, where the fast-flowing water does not freeze.

The **CREEK TRAIL** (2 miles) joins Bowser's Resort and Anderson's Outfitters. Skiing from Bowser's, the trail first passes through a stand of big, old aspens, then crosses Camp 40 Creek and enters a forest of primarily new growth. The trail slopes gently downhill from Anderson's toward Crane Lake. When snow and ice conditions are favorable, Camp 40 Creek offers a good alternative route that intersects the Creek Trail.

The **CLIFF TRAIL** (1 mile) extends from the intersection of Forest Route 491 (Vermilion Falls Road) and County Road 24 to the southern-most bay of Crane Lake. It is nearly level most of the way, but ends with a fast "caution hill" down to the Handberg Road and the shore of the lake. There was once a gold mine in the spectacular cliffs that border the west side of the trail.

Using the secondary trails, creeks and lake surfaces, loops of almost any duration may be added to the primary trails. The Crane Lake Tower Trail extends west from the Neighborhood Trails. An ambitious skier may even plot a course that joins Crane Lake with the Herriman Lake Trails. With prior arrangements, the local snowmobile club members will set a ski track on any of the trails in advance of a tour.

FOR MORE INFORMATION: Contact the Crane Lake Commercial Club, Crane Lake, MN 55725. Or phone (218) 993-2346 for current snow conditions.

A Voyageur greets visitors to the Crane Lake area.

Crane Lake Tower Ski Trail

Use Level: Light

Trail Type: Machine groomed

Difficulty: Intermediate

Trail Length: 4 miles

Connects to: Crane Lake Neighborhood Trails

Maps: Available at local resorts

Highlights: Panoramic vistas from bare ledgerock

Trailhead: At Voyaguaire Houseboats

Description: The Crane Lake Tower Trail combines the contrasting appeal of skiing on high, open ridges and in low, meandering creeks. The first half of this loop affords skiers panoramic views from atop a ridge that connects the Gorge Trail (part of the Crane Lake Neighborhood Trails) with one of the highest points in the area — the site of the Crane Lake Lookout Tower. The view from the base of the abandoned tower is breathtaking. Large trees in a forest dominated by evergreens line the trail, which parallels the Voyageur Snowmobile Trail part of the way. From the west end of the trail, skiers may either 1) backtrack to their origin, 2) follow the Vermilion Falls Road (unplowed in winter) to County Road 24, or 3) ski on Camp 40 Creek back to the Crane Lake Neighborhood Trails. When ice and snow are favorable, the creek option is the most interesting alternative.

At a point ½ mile from the trailhead, skiers may take a one-mile side-trip down to the Vermilion River gorge (See The Crane Lake Neighborhood Trails).

FOR MORE INFORMATION: Contact the Crane Lake Commercial Club, Crane Lake, MN 55725. Or phone (218) 993-2346 for current snow conditions.

The scenic Vermilion Gorge is accessible from the Crane Lake Tower Trail.

Partridge Falls cascades 40 feet into a scenic, rocky gorge — a popular destination for skiers at Grand Portage Reservation.

VOYAGEUR COUNTRY LODGING

Winter lodging accommodations in Voyageur Country are grouped into five geographic "neighborhoods" — the Cook area, the Crane Lake area, the Lake Kabetogama area, the Orr area and the Rainy Lake area. Nearby International Falls (not included in this guide, because it falls outside of St. Louis' County) also offers a host of motels and restaurants to visitors in this region. For more information about any of these "neighborhoods," contact one or more of the resort associations or chambers of commerce that are listed in the introduction to this chapter.

The COOK Area

ELBOW LAKE LODGE
OWNER/MANAGER: The Ranta Family
ADDRESS: P.O. Box 136, Cook, MN 55723
PHONE: (218) 666-2631
LODGING: 1 Housekeeping Cabin
AMENITIES: Lodge with fireplace; games and TV

COMMENTS: Elbow Lake Lodge currently offers the only winterized lodging facility in the Cook area. Resting on the east shore of Elbow Lake, the lodge is 13 miles north of Cook and the only resort on that lake. There is a 2½-mile groomed ski trail adjacent to the lodge, and skiers have direct access to the proposed 39-mile Ashawa Ski Trail around the west end of Lake Vermilion.

Elbow Lake Lodge. (Photo compliments of Ray Ranta)

MELGEORGE'S RESORT
OWNER/MANAGER: Ted Melgeorge
ADDRESS: Box 185, Orr, MN 55771
PHONE: (218) 374-3621
LODGING: 8 motel units each accommodate 6 people
DINING: Restaurant and lounge
COMMENTS: Melgeorge's Resort is located on Elephant Lake, 10 miles north-east of Cusson on County Road 180. There are 3 miles of groomed ski trails adjacent to the resort, available for use by guests.

The CRANE LAKE Area

BOWSER'S RESORT
OWNER/MANAGER:
ADDRESS: Route 3 Box 72, Crane Lake, MN 55725
PHONE: (218) 993-2226 or -2213
LODGING: Motel units, and lodge rooms
COMMENTS: Located at the south end of Crane Lake, the accommodations at Bowser's Resort all have bathrooms, and there are some cooking units in the motel. Housekeeping cabins are not open during the winter season.

CRANE LAKE BASE CAMP
OWNER/MANGER: Jeff and Joni Wartchow
ADDRESS: Crane Lake, MN 55725
PHONE: (218) 993-2396
LODGING: Housekeeping cabin with 3 bedrooms
AMENITIES: Sauna; laundry
COMMENTS: The Overnighter is a lodge-type facility at Crane Lake Base Camp that provides guests with thoroughly modern lodging accommodations. Located at the south end of Crane Lake, it is only a couple of miles north of the Herriman Lake Trail and has direct access to Voyageurs National Park. There are plans for expansion of the winter operation in the future.

The Overnighter is a lodge-type facility at Crane Lake Base Camp.

OLSON'S BORDERLAND LODGE

OWNER/MANAGER: Joan and Larry Olson
ADDRESS: Box 310, Crane Lake, MN 55725
PHONE: (218) 993-2233
LODGING: 1-3 bedroom Housekeeping cabins, and motel rooms in the Lodge.
DINING: Full-service restaurant, open to the public
AMENITIES: Sauna; laundromat; grocery store
COMMENTS: Sitting at the southern tip of Crane lake, at the entrance to Voyageurs National Park, Olson's Borderland Lodge provides skiers with completely modern accommodations. The Herriman Lake Trail system is only two miles south, and there are numerous local trails in the immediate Crane Lake Area.

Olson's Borderland Lodge sits near the entrance to Voyageurs National Park.

LAKE KABETOGAMA Area

DRIFTWOOD LODGE

OWNER/MANAGER: Norm and Treva Bonam
ADDRESS: Ray, MN 56669
PHONE: (218) 875-3841
LODGING: Housekeeping cabins
AMENITIES: Main lodge with large recreation and TV room; grocery store
COMMENTS: Located three miles off of Highway 53 on the southwest shore of Kabetogama Lake. Driftwood Lodge offers 16 rustic housekeeping cabins, some with showers. A central shower facility is located near the lodge. The facility is open year-round.

PINE AIRE RESORT

OWNER/MANAGER: Sherwood and Chris Anderson
ADDRESS: Box 80, Ray, MN 56669
PHONE: (218) 875-2161
LODGING: 8 lakeside cabins
AMENITIES: Recreation building and bar
COMMENTS: Pine Aire Resort sits on the south shore of Kabetogama Lake, near the Visitors' Center at the entrance to Voyageurs National Park.

SUNSET RESORT

OWNER/MANAGER: Mark and Lynette Hraban
ADDRESS: Ash River Trail, Orr, MN 55771
PHONE: (218) 374-3161
LODGING: 4 large modern housekeeping cabins; American Plan available
DINING: Restaurant and bar, open to the public
AMENITIES: Lodge with recreation equipment
COMMENTS: Sunset Resort rests on the scenic shore of the Ash River, near the east end of Kabetogama Lake and the heart of Voyageurs National Park. The Ash River Recreation Trail is less than five miles away, and there are hundreds of square miles of untracked wilderness sitting just to the north. Snowmobiles are available for rent.

KEC'S KOVE

OWNER/MANAGER: Al and Gen Kec, Larry and Viv Kec
ADDRESS: Ray, MN 56669
PHONE: (218) 875-2841
LODGING: Housekeeping cabins
DINING: Public restaurant and cocktail lounge, open for lunches and dinners.
AMENITIES: Recreation room; TV in the Lodge
COMMENTS: Kec's Kove offers modern cottages, most with fireplaces, that are completely furnished for housekeeping. Located on Kabetogama Lake, only seven miles from Highway 53, the Lodge sits on the southwest edge of Voyageurs National Park. Weekend "packages" are available that include meals.

ROCKY POINT RESORT

OWNER/MANAGER: Barb and Garrett Rasmussen
ADDRESS: P.O. Box 183 LA, Ray, MN 56669
PHONE: (218) 875-2411
LODGING: 1 housekeeping cabin and 2 motel units above the Lodge
DINING: Full bar and restaurant open on weekends: American Plan and Modified American Plan available.
COMMENTS: Rocky Point Resort is located near the west end of Kabetogama Lake, on the edge of Voyageurs National Park.

RAINY LAKE Area

THUNDERBIRD LODGE

OWNER/MANAGER: Stanley W. Wyman
ADDRESS: Island View Route, International Falls, MN 56649
PHONE: (218) 286-3151
LODGING: Housekeeping cabins and motel units in the main lodge
DINING: Restaurant and Lounge open on weekends to the public
AMENITIES: Color TV in the lodge guest rooms
COMMENTS: Located ten miles east of International Falls, Thunderbird Lodge sits on the south shore of Rainy Lake, at the western entrance to Voyageurs National Park, near the Black Bay Ski Trail. The dining room and lounge are available to guests, staying in the lodge, by reservation only, during the week.

CHAPTER 10

THE RANGE

As the United States is the cultural "melting pot" of the world, the Range is one of the finest examples of this phenomenon. Immigrants from Sweden, Finland, Italy, Jugoslavia and other eastern Europoean countries settled in this region at the turn of this century. And ethnic traditions, languages, customs and foods are still quite evident today.

Many of the residents make their living either directly or indirectly from the mining industry. Built around various iron ore mines in the late 1800's and early 1900's, mining and processing of iron ore has since been a mainstay of the area's economy. Until the late 1950's, the mining of high grade natural ores prevailed on the Iron Range. When high grade ore bodies began to become depleted, a process was developed for extracting iron from taconite. Millions of tons of taconite pellets are extracted each year on America's largest iron range.

More than a dozen towns grew up around the mines, and now most of the Arrowhead's population (north of Duluth) is found on the Range. Population centers are found at Aurora, Babbitt, Biwabik, Buhl, Calumet, Chisholm, Eveleth, Gilbert, Hibbing, Hoyt Lakes, Keewatin, Mountain Iron, Tower-Soudan and Virginia. A full complement of lodging accommodations and dining and shopping facilities are available in the Range communities.

Hosting our nation's best cross country skiers, Giants Ridge Ski Area (near Biwabik) is an official training center for the U.S. Ski Association. And, for the weekend gliders, there are over 130 miles of designated ski trails on the Range, most of which are machine groomed and track-set. A splendid variety of trails will satisfy all types of skiers, beginners to experts.

In addition to a tantalizing assortment of cross country trails, the Range offers visitors a remarkably diversified list of attractions. Included are the United States Hockey Hall of Fame (Eveleth), the Iron Range Interpretative Center (Chisholm), the Paulucci Planetarium (Hibbing), the First Settlers Museum (Hibbing), the world's largest open pit iron ore mine (Hull Rust Mahoning Mine, Hibbing), Minnesota's oldest and deepest iron ore mine (Tower-Soudan), and the "Mardi Gras of the North Winter Festival" (Virginia). There is plenty to see and do on the Range after the skis are hung up for the night.

City of Tower Ski Trail

Use Level: Moderate

Trail Type: Machine groomed and track-set

Difficulty: Beginner, Intermediate and Advanced

Trail Length: 6 miles

Maps: Stocked in a box at the trailhead

Highlights: Beautiful forest of Norway Pine; good chance to see deer and small game

Trailhead: Parking lot on the west side of Highway 135, 1½ miles south of Tower.

Description: The Tower Ski Trail consists of a variety of loops that are appropriately marked according to the skill level required. They are maintained and groomed by the Vermilion Ski Touring Club. Most of the single-tracked loops have one-way directional signs, but there is a two-way intermediate trail that connects the loops with another trailhead in the town of Tower, near the junction of Highways 1 and 135.

The trails pass over a good variety of terrain, mostly suitable for intermediate skiers, although there are a couple small loops that beginners will enjoy and some difficult segments for advanced skiers. A lovely forest of red pine harbors deer and small game, affording skiers a good chance to view wildlife.

Bearhead Lake State Park

Use Level: Moderate

Trail Type: Machine groomed and track-set

Difficulty: All skill levels, beginner to advanced

Trail Length: 17 miles

Connects to: The Taconite State Trail

Maps: Brochure with map available from Park Ranger

Highlights: Good Wildlife area; excellent trails

Trailhead: 18 miles east of Tower. From Tower, drive east on Highway 169 12 miles to St. Louis County Highway 128. Turn right and drive 6 miles south to the park entrance.

Description: Some of the nicest ski trails in the area are found in Bearhead Lake State Park. The 4000-acre park surrounds Bearhead Lake, includes several other smaller lakes and is bordered by Eagles Nest Lake No. 3 on the north. Across the northern part of the park is the Taconite State Trail, a multiple-use trail that extends all the way from Ely to Grand Rapids. Skiers and snowmobilers share the 4½ mile portion of the trail that passes through the park, as well as 1 1½-mile spur trail from the parking area to the Taconite Trail. But there are several loops reserved exclusively for skiers.

Wildlife abounds in this area. A large population of white-tailed deer congregates here year-round, and moose are occasionally seen in the park. Consequently timber wolves also frequent the park. In 1986, a lynx was also seen in the park.

As in all state parks, a state park sticker is required for vehicles entering the park (except snowmobiles). The annual fee is $15, or a daily fee of $3 may be paid. Minnesota ski permits are also required (see page 35 for information), and they may be purchased at the park headquarters.

Bearhead Lake State Park offers some of the best trails in the whole region. Prior to the Ely-to-Tower Wilderness Trek and Loppet each winter, ski racers are often seen training on the more difficult trails in the park.

There are trails for all skill levels. The easiest loops for beginning skiers are located in and around the campgrounds, along the north shore of Bearhead Lake. The most challenging loop, designated for experts, is the 2-mile trail around Becky Lake. Most of the other trails pass over gently rolling terrain that is ideally suited for intermediate skiers. The 2-mile loop around Norberg Lake affords a delightful journey through impressive stands of huge red and white pines, with a couple of nice downhill runs along the way.

FOR MORE INFORMATION: Contact the Park Manager, Bearhead Lake State Park, Star Route 2, Box 5700, Ely, MN 55731. Or phone (218) 365-4253 for current snow conditions.

Some of the nicest ski trails in area are found in Bearhead Lake State Park.

A park map directs skiers to a delightful journey around Norberg Lake.

"Birch Run" is one of the prettiest parts of the Bird Lake Trails.

The Lillian Lake Loop is an excellent course for beginning skiers.

Bird Lake Trails

Use Level: Light to moderate

Trail Type: Machine groomed and track-set

Difficulty: Trails for all skill levels (mostly beginner and intermediate)

Trail Length: 18 miles

Maps: "Recreation Opportunity Guide" Available from the Aurora Ranger District, United States Forest Service, or at the trailheads.

Highlights: Excellent variety of forest habitats; some nice downhill runs

Trailhead: The trail system has two major access points: at the Bird Lake picnic grounds, about 5 miles southeast of Hoyt Lakes, and at the east end of Hoyt Lakes. To reach the Bird Lake trailhead, drive east from Hoyt Lakes trailhead on County Highway 565 for .7 mile to its junction with County Road 569. Turn right and drive southeast on 569 4.1 miles to the picnic grounds at Bird Lake. There are parking areas at both trailheads.

Description: This 18-mile network of trails connects the town of Hoyt Lakes with Bird Lake, crossing an interesting variety of Northwoods landscape. Rolling hills covered with aspen and birch, dense stands of black spruce in the lowlands, and open bogs are all parts of a skier's experience. There is enough beauty and variety in the vegetation and the terrain (even on those stretches rated "easy") to eliminate the possibility of boredom or monotony.

The "corridor trail" that connects Hoyt Lakes with Bird Lake is an easy trail that parallels County Road 569 most of the way. Likewise, the **ST. LOUIS RIVER LOOP** offers a nearly level course, crossing over a large bog and Hush Lake en route to the St. Louis River. It's a good route for beginners and racers who want to kick up a storm.

The **LILLIAN LAKE LOOPS,** south of the Bird Lake Picnic grounds, are relatively easy trails for intermediate skiers. There is an Adirondak-type shelter for skiers on the loop directly south of Lillian Lake. The **BIRD LAKE LOOPS,** north of County Road 569, cross hillier terrain that offers a challenge to more experienced skiers. Although most of the loops are appropriate for intermediate skiers, there are a couple short trail segments that are classified "most difficult." Birch Run, at the northeast end of the system, is considered a particularly pretty part of the trail. It passes through a lovely, pure stand of paper birch.

All of the trails are expertly groomed and track-set by a group of volunteers working in cooperation with the Forest Service. The citizens of Hoyt Lakes are fortunate to have such a fine system of ski trails in their own "backyard." And visitors to the Arrowhead will not regret making the trip to this little-known Ski Country gem.

FOR MORE INFORMATION: Contact the Aurora District Ranger, United States Forest Service, Box 391, Aurora, Minnesota 55705. Or call (218) 229-3371 for current snow conditions.

The 12,000-square-foot chalet at Giants Ridge contains a restaurant, bar and ski rental shop.

Racers train on excellent trails at Giants Ridge — one of the best groomed networks in the Arrowhead.

The Bronze Trail provides a long downhill run for inexperienced skiers at Giants Ridge.

Giants Ridge Ski Area

Use Level: Heavy

Trail Type: Machine groomed and track-set

Difficulty: Beginner, intermediate and advanced

Trail Length: 25 miles

Maps: Available at Lodge

Highlights: Outstanding panorama; excellent groomed trails

Location: Giants Ridge is located about four miles (by air) northeast of Biwabik, twelve miles northeast of Virginia. From Biwabik, drive east via Highway 135 to the well-marked turn-off. Turn left (north) there, and proceed on a good gravel road for three miles to Giants Ridge.

Fees: Trail use fees vary, depending on the day of the week and the time of the day. Weekdays and nighttime skiing cost the least. On weekends and holidays, those rates increase. Children under age six may ski free with one paid adult. Season passes are also available. Equipment rentals are also available.

Description: Giants Ridge is one of the newest, and one of the best, Nordic ski centers in Minnesota. Owned and operated by the Iron Range Resource and Rehabilitation Board (I.R.R.R.B.). the $7,000,000 project was constructed in 1984 and opened for the 1984-85 ski season. In addition to providing recreational skiers with some of the finest (and best groomed) trails in the midwest, Giants Ridge is also the official United States Ski Association Midwest Nordic Training Facility. A 30-position biathlon range is also part of the layout. In all, there are 25 miles of cross country trails that were designed by Al Merrill, the man who designed Olympic competition trails at Squaw Valley, Lake Placid and Calgary. A Pisten-Bully grooming machine and double Bachler track setter create perfect tracks.

Giants Ridge straddles the Laurentian Highlands — the north-south continental divide. At the summit of the alpine slopes, an incredible panorama exists. In spring, the fate of melting snow will be determined by gravity. Snow melting on the north and west side of the divide will eventually drain into the Arctic Ocean, while water on the south and east side of this geologic barrier will end up in the Atlantic Ocean. White birch is dominant in these Laurentian Highlands. Its blend with the conifers provides an interesting, and lovely, contrast for cross-country skiers.

A 12,000 square foot chalet contains a 250-seat restaurant, a separate bar, a rental shop, and a wall full of windows, where one may relax in warmth while viewing alpine skiers on the downhill slopes. Not far from the chalet is a dormitory that may house up to 50 athletes who train year-round at the facility. Weight training and sports medicine facilities adjoin the Nordic accommodations.

Essentially, there are two trail heads at Giants Ridge. One is located just north of the chalet, and it provides access to the SILVER TRAIL, the LAURENTIAN TRAIL and the NORTHERN LIGHTS TRAIL. The other is 450 feet above the chalet, at the top of the main chair lift, providing access to the BRONZE TRAIL and the GOLD TRAIL. One chair lift is included with the price of the trails.

The **BRONZE TRAIL** (3 miles): The easiest of the five trails, it follows a gradual downhill slope for the first two miles. The final mile crosses gently rolling terrain, where several steep, but short, slopes are encountered. To enjoy a very pleasant downhill run, take the lift to the summit and ski back down to the chalet. For those who don't mind skiing up a gradual slope, start at the chalet and ski to the top and back down, a total distance of slightly more than six miles. About ¾ of your time will be spent on the uphill grade, and the return trip is a "breeze." Even though this is the EASIEST trail at Giants Ridge, it may be a bit too challenging for beginners who haven't quite mastered hills. The Bronze Trail is for advanced beginners and intermediates.

The **GOLD TRAIL** (9.3 miles): The most difficult of the five trails, the Gold Trail was designed primarily with a World Cup Ski Race in mind, according to Peter Graves, Nordic Director. It challenges the steep slopes of the Laurentian Divide. The Gold Trail is accessible from either trail head, but those who just can't wait for the steep downhill runs should head straight for the chair lift and begin their adventure at the top of the 450-foot ridge. From the top, skiers have a choice of loops heading east or west, or they may ski down to the other trail head and join up with one or more of the other three trails. Beginners and intermediates should avoid this trail, and advanced skiers should approach it with caution. Experts will love the exciting challenge!

The **SILVER TRAIL** (6.2 miles): In terms of difficulty, the Silver Trail falls between the Gold and Bronze trails. Giants Ridge officials label it "more difficult," a good challenge for intermediate and advanced skiers. Beginning at the trail head just north of the chalet, the Silver Trail winds through a terrain of small hills, with occasional steep slopes. "It requires good technical skiing skills and a lot of up and down terrain and quick and technical corners," according to Graves. It doesn't have the length of hills that the Gold Trail enjoys.

The **NORTHERN LIGHTS LOOP** (2.2 miles): The only lighted trail for night skiing, the Northern Lights Loop passes through much of the same rolling terrain through which the Silver Trail passes. Where the Silver Trail tackles a steep grade straight on, however, the Northern Lights Loop generally follows an easier grade. Nevertheless, beginners will have difficulty on much of the trail, even though it is considered "easier" by Giants Ridge officials. This route is more challenging than the Bronze Trail. Be prepared to herringbone or side-step up some of the steeper slopes.

The **LAURENTIAN TRAIL** (3.7 miles round-trip): Suitable for beginners and intermediates, the Laurentian Trail begins at the trail head just north of the chalet and passes through gentle terrain and the intersecting web of trails located north of the Alpine Mountains. It extends almost 2 miles up to its intersection with a snowmobile trail. At that point, skiers must backtrack to a point where they may join either the Silver or the Northern Lights trails.

FOR MORE INFORMATION: Contact the Giants Ridge Ski Area, Box 190, Biwabik, MN 55708. Or call (218) 865-4143 or (800) 262-SNOW.

America's best cross country skiers compete in biathlon competitions at Giants Ridge.

Skiers are treated to a splendid panorama atop the Giant's Ridge.

A chair lift carries skiers to the top of the Bronze and Gold trails at Giants Ridge Ski Area.

Potential hazards are well-padded at Giants Ridge.

A large Forest Service map guides visitors to the Big Aspen Ski Trails.

The Big Aspen Ski Trails lead through — what else? — dense stands of large aspen trees.

Big Aspen Ski Trails

Use Level: Moderate to Heavy

Trail Type: Machine groomed and track-set

Difficulty: Trails for all skill levels, beginner to advanced.

Trail Length: 22 miles

Maps: Available from the Virginia District Ranger, United States Forest Service, and at the trailhead

Highlights: Many scenic overlooks

Trailhead: 11 miles north of Virginia, along Forest Route 257. From the intersection of Highways 169 and 53 in Virginia, drive north on Highway 53 for 7.7 miles to County Road 302, which veers off to the right. Continue driving north on 302 for .9 mile to County Road 68. Turn left and follow 68 for .3 mile to County Road 405, which veers to the right on a gravel road. Follow County Road 405 northwest for 2.1 miles to the trailhead at the junction of Forest Routes 257 and 256. Parking is available on the left (west) side of the road. Two trails begin on the opposite side of the road.

Description: The Big Aspen area is a maze of interconnected loops that extend east and northwest from the main parking lot at the end of County Road 405. Because of its close proximity to the larger Range Cities, it receives quite a bit of use on weekends, although weekday use is normally light. The trails lead through a variety of tree species in various stages of growth, affording an interesting look at Superior National Forest.

Most of the loops and all of the more challenging trails weave throughout the northwestern part of the Big Aspen area. Access to this area begins in an aspen forest at the north side of the intersection of Forest Routes 256 and 257, following an intermediate-level trail north to the area. On the south side of Forest Route 256 and the east side of County Road 405 is the beginning of an easy trail system that is recommended for beginning skiers. It begins in a stand of Norway pines and extends east and south to form three loops. At the north end of the easternmost loop is a 1¼-mile connecting trail that leads north to the other trail network. It descends on a long, gentle aspen-covered slope, crosses Forest Road 256, and then enters a vast open region that was recently logged over.

There are two log shelters and many scenic overlooks along the trails in the northwestern part of the system. Most loops range from easy to intermediate in difficulty, but there are some challenging trails for expert skiers in the northwesternmost part of the system. Beware a couple of big, steep hills that require caution by experienced skiers and should be avoided alltogether by those with little experience.

All of the trails are nicely groomed and track-set. Intersections are clearly marked with numbers or letters that are keyed to the map, which allows easy navigation through the maze of interconnected loops.

FOR MORE INFORMATION: Contact the Virginia Ranger District, United States Forest Service, 505 12th Avenue West, Virginia, MN 55792. Or call (218) 741-5736 for current snow conditions.

HUDSON BAY

LAKE SUPERIOR

LAURENTIAN DIVIDE

SUPERIOR NATIONAL FOREST

The Laurentian Divide is the ridge of low, rugged hills meandering through Northern Minnesota that separates the headwaters of streams which flow North and South. Streams which begin on the North slope of the Divide flow through Canada to Hudson Bay and the Arctic Ocean.

On the opposite side of the divide, streams flow South into Lake Superior, eventually reaching the Atlantic Ocean. The Laurentian Divide, at this location, is only a remnant of a once gigantic mountain range formed more than a billion years ago.

A BILLION YEARS AGO

FOREST SERVICE
U.S. DEPARTMENT OF AGRICULTURE

The Lookout Mountain Ski Trails loop across the north-south Continental Divide.

Lookout Mountain Ski Trail

Use Level: Heavy

Trail Type: Mostly machine groomed and track-set

Difficulty: Intermediate to advanced

Trail Length: 14.7 miles

Maps: Available from the Virginia District Ranger, United States Forest Service

Highlights: Challenging loops for good skiers

Trailhead: At the Laurentian Divide Rest Stop along Highways 53 and 169, 4 miles north of the junction of those two highways in Virginia.

Description: This concentrated network of trail loops sits atop the Laurentian Highlands — the north-south continental divide. Melting snow on the north side of the divide eventually winds up in the Arctic Ocean, while run-off on the south-facing slopes works its way toward the Atlantic Ocean. Though not as dramatic as the east-west divide that forms the spine of the Rocky Mountains, the Laurentian Divide is, nevertheless, a significant ridge that slices across northeastern Minnesota. It is the remnant of a mountain range that was formed over a billion years ago.

As one might expect, because of its close proximity to the city of Virginia, the Lookout Mountain Trails receive a good deal of use on weekends, although weekday use is on the light side. The trails are maintained by the Laurentian Nordic Ski Club, an organization based in Virginia.

Three trails originate at the parking lot. The middle one is for snowmobiles, providing access to the Laurentian Snowmobile Trail, which skirts the northern rim of the ski area. The ski trail at the north end of the rest area leads further north to the easiest ski trail in the area. It parallels the snowmobile trail east for 2 miles and then loops back into the hillier central part of the area, rated for intermediate skiers.

The southernmost trail stemming from the parking lot leads more directly to the "more difficult" loops in the southern part of the system near Lookout Mountain. The "most difficult" trails lie at the easternmost end of the system. A three-sided shelter hut is located at a scenic overlook on the eastern loop, which makes a good destination for competent skiers.

Although certain portions of this trail system are fairly easy, the beginning skier will have difficulty completing any loop. The trails are basically for intermediate and expert skiers.

FOR MORE INFORMATION: Contact the Virginia District Ranger, United States Forest Service, 505 12th Avenue West, Virginia, MN 55792. Or call (218) 741-5736 for current snow conditions.

Sturgeon River Ski Trail

Use Level: Light

Trail Type: Not often groomed

Difficulty: Mostly intermediate

Trail Length: 20 miles

Maps: Available from the Virginia District Ranger, United States Forest Service.

Highlights: Sturgeon River landscape and ecology

Trailhead: Located approximately 10-15 miles north of Chisholm, there are three access points: 1) The junction of State Highways 73 and County Road 791, ten miles north of Chisholm; 2) 1.3 miles west of Highway 73 on County Road 65, which intersects Highway 73 thirteen miles north of Chisholm; or 3) 15½ miles north of Chisholm on State Highway 73.

Description: The Sturgeon River Trail is one of the most extensive trail systems in the Virginia Ranger District. It is also the newest and least used trail. Because of its length, there are sections for all types of skiers, from beginner to expert, though most is for intermediate-level skiers.

The trail parallels the Sturgeon River, where unique vegetation and topographic relief provide interesting scenery for skiers. The trail generally follows gently rolling terrain adjacent to high, steep slopes that descend to the river. Open water will be seen on parts of the river.

The trail leads through an interesting mixture of forest habitats, including mature pine stands, stands of young aspen, meadows, and timber clearcut areas resulting from recent logging activity. Large, old-growth silver maples line the flood plain. Ruffed grouse, deer and coyote are known to inhabit the area.

A loop around Jean Lake, at the south end of the system, is quite steep. It is recommended only for experienced skiers. An Adirondack-type shelter is located on the east shore of the lake. A similar shelter sits along the north-central part of the trail, north of County Road 65.

The trail is not groomed often. And, since it receives very little use, skiers may have to break trail. In the spring of 1986, when this volume was published, the northern part of the trail system was not yet completed. Nor was the section along the East Branch of the river. The entire trail system, as well as a new parking lot at the junction of Highway 73 and Forest Route 279, should be completed soon, however. In the meantime, the Forest Service will supply a map showing which parts of the trail are complete and which are incomplete.

The trail crosses County Road 65, Forest Road 179, and Highway 73. Use caution at these points.

FOR MORE INFORMATION: Contact the Virginia Ranger District, United States Forest Service, 505 12th Avenue West, Virginia, MN 55792. Or call (218) 741-5736 for current snow conditions.

The Sturgeon River Trail follows a high ridge overlooking the scenic Sturgeon River.

McCarthy Beach State Park

Use Level: Moderate

Trail Type: Machine groomed and track-set

Difficulty: All skill levels, beginner through advanced

Trail Length: 8.4 miles of groomed trails

Connects to: The Taconite State Trail

Maps: Brochure with map available from Park Manager

Highlights: 30-acre designated trout lake; virgin pine

Trailhead: From the junction of Highways 5 and 169, one mile west of Highway 73 in Chisholm, drive north on County Road 5 for 15.4 miles to County Road #65. Turn left and drive 1.1 miles to the Park Ranger's office.

Description: McCarthy Beach State Park's trail system consists primarily of two groomed and tracked loops with access trails. One loop is 3.6 miles in length, and the other is 2 miles. Another 1.2 mile ungroomed trail encircles Pickerel Lake, a 30-acre designated trout lake that is very popular with winter anglers. All of the trails wind through ridges and valleys forested with Norway pine, white pine and birch.

The park is bordered on the south and west by Side, Sturgeon and Beatrice lakes, and more than half a dozen smaller lakes are located in the park's interior. White-tailed deer and timber wolves inhabit the park, as well as a variety of smaller wildlife.

In addition to the specified cross-country ski trails, there are also 12 miles of snowmobile trails and access to the Taconite State Trail, a multiple-use trail that stretches for 165 miles between Ely and Grand Rapids. Skiing is permitted on multiple-use trails, but they are not track-set for skiers.

Trailheads are located adjacent to the Park Ranger's office and also at a point 1.1 miles north of the office, just west of Pickerel Lake. Between the trailhead and Pickerel Lake, the trail is used more by trout anglers and snowmobiles than by skiers. After about ¼ mile, however, the ski trail branches off the multiple-use trail. At that point, there is a self-registration station where visitors are asked to report in.

Use levels in the park range from light on weekdays to heavy during holiday periods. Normal weekend use, however, is moderate. Food, gas, lodging and spirits are available within a mile of the trail access points, and rental skis are available locally. As at all state parks, park permits are required for vehicles. Daily ($3) or annual ($15) permits may be purchased at park headquarters upon arrival.

FOR MORE INFORMATION: Contact the Park Manager, McCarthy Beach State Park, Star Route 2, Hibbing, MN 55746. Or call (218) 254-2411 for current snow conditions.

Pickerel Lake is a popular destination for trout fishermen visiting McCarthy Beach State Park.

A self-registration station is found at the beginning of ski trails leading into McCarthy Beach State Park.

Hibbing Municipal Trails

The Hibbing Joint Recreation and Park Board maintains over six miles of groomed cross country ski trails within the city of Hibbing. All of the trails are suitable for beginning skiers and are designed to be skied in one direction only, marked with directional arrows. Hiking, sledding, snowshoeing, snowmobiling and dogs are not allowed on the trails. Ski rentals are available at the Vic Power Park shelter building. In addition to the ski trails, the Board also sponsors seven ice skating and hockey rinks with warming shelters, eight neighborhood ice skating rinks, and a tubing slide.

FOR MORE INFORMATION: Contact the Hibbing Joint Recreation and Park Board, Memorial Building, Hibbing, MN 55746. Or call the office at (218) 263-8851.

Vic Power Park Trail

Use Level: Moderate

Trail Type: Machine groomed and track-set

Difficulty: Beginner

Trail Length: West Loop = 1½ miles; Combined East and West Loops = 2 miles

Maps: Available at the Joint Recreation and Park Board office. Memorial Building, Hibbing, MN 55746

Trailhead: Vic Power Park is located approximately ½ mile east of Highway 169 on 25th Street in Hibbing.

Description: The Vic Power Park Trail starts at the heated shelter building in the north side of the park, and it follows the perimeter of the park for a total distance of about 2 miles. The newly expanded West Loop is 1½ miles long. Both loops are geared primarily for the beginning skier. Concessions, ski rentals and satellites are available at the park. Group ski rentals are also available.

Cross country skis and other gear may be rented at Vic Power Park in Hibbing.

211

Rest stop along the
Carey Lake Trail.

The Carey Lake Trail passes through a dense stand of jackpines.

Carey Lake Trail

Use Level: Moderate

Trail Type: Machine groomed and track-set

Difficulty: Beginner

Trail Length: North Loop = 2 miles; Combined North and South Loops = 3½ miles

Maps: Available at the Joint Recreation and Park Board office, Memorial Building, Hibbing, MN 55746.

Trailhead: On the north side of 25th Street (Dupont Road), approximately ¼ mile before the park entrance gate, 3½ miles east of Highway 169.

Description: Located in the 1100-acre Carey Lake Park, the trail runs through primarily lowlands and spruce bogs, with about ⅓ of the trail on high land. Skiers have the option of skiing only the North Loop, a distance of 2 miles, or combining the North and South Loops for a total distance of 3½ miles.

RANGE AREA LODGING

All of the winter lodging facilities in the Range area are motels located in the various Range towns, from Aurora to Hibbing. Although not associated directly with particular ski areas, all are within easy access to one or more of the ski areas described in this guide. And, because of their urban locations, there are a host of amenities — restaurants, laundries, bars and other recreation — located nearby.

AURORA

AURORA PINES MOTEL: Maureen Krsiean, Manager
ADDRESS: 310 West 1st Avenue South, Aurora, MN 55705
PHONE: (218) 229-3377
ACCOMMODATIONS: 20 large rooms, cable TV, plug-ins for car heaters, kitchenettes available
COMMENTS: Within walking distance of downtown shopping and restaurants. The Aurora Pines Motel sits in a quiet residential neighborhood, only 5 miles from Giant's Ridge. Shuttle bus service to the ski area is offered.

The Aurora Pines Motel rests in a quiet residential neighborhood, only minutes away from Giant's Ridge Ski Area.

SKI-VIEW MOTEL:
ADDRESS: 903 North 17th Street
PHONE: (218) 741-8918
ACCOMMODATIONS: 59 spacious rooms, color cable TV Showtime, direct-dial telephones, plug-ins for car heaters, sauna, continental breakfast included.
COMMENTS: Located near the north edge of Virginia. Special discounts for skiers. Located 20 minutes from Giants Ridge.

VOYAGEUR NORTH MOTEL
ADDRESS: 13th Street and Hwy 53, Virginia, MN 55792
PHONE: (218) 741-9235
ACCOMMODATIONS: 18 large rooms, color cable TV with HBO, plug-ins for car heaters, free continental breakfast.
COMMENTS: Voyageur North Motel offers group rates and ski packages, as well as discount coupons for use at the Giant's Ridge Ski Area. Shuttle bus service is also offered to the ski area.

The **EVELETH-VIRGINIA AREA MOTEL ASSOCIATION** lists the following additional motels and resorts that offer ski packages and shuttle service to Giant's Ridge Ski Area:
BIWABIK MOTEL, Biwabik
CLOUD NINE MOTEL, Virginia
COATES PLAZA HOTEL, Virginia
HALF MOON LAKE ROADHOUSE AND RESORT, Eveleth
HOLIDAY INN, Eveleth
LAKESHORE MOTOR INN, Virginia
MIDWAY MOTEL, Virginia
NORTHERN MOTEL, Virginia
SLOVENE MOTEL, Eveleth
STARFIRE MOTEL, Virginia

HIBBING-CHISHOLM

REGENCY INN: Sandy Hautala, Manager

ADDRESS: 1402 E. Howard Street, Hibbing, MN 55746

PHONE: (218) 262-3481

ACCOMMODATIONS: 125 rooms, color cable TV, direct-dial telephones, room service, conference rooms, restaurant and bar; live entertainment.

OTHER AMENITIES: Swimming pool, sauna, children's play area, video games, babysitting service, lobby with newsstand and sundries.

COMMENTS: The Regency Inn is a deluxe facility located near the north end of Hibbing, on Highway 169. The Brass Wings Restaurant is open to the public seven days a week and offers a complete menu.

SCOTWOOD MOTEL: Steven Kopp, Manager

ADDRESS: Highway 169, Box 552, Chisholm, MN 55719

PHONE: (218) 254-3393

ACCOMMODATIONS: Spacious rooms, color TV, free continental breakfast, 10% discount at the adjacent Country Kitchen Restaurant.

COMMENTS: Scotwood Motels are known for their clean rooms, friendly hospitality and economical rates.

THRIFTY SCOT MOTEL:

ADDRESS: 1526 Highway 37 East, Box 662, Hibbing, MN 55746

PHONE: (218) 263-8306

ACCOMMODATIONS: 100 rooms, color TV, free local phone, free continental breakfast, facilities accessible to the handicapped.

COMMENTS: Located at the southeast edge of Hibbing, the motel offers clean, comfortable rooms at competitive prices. It is adjacent to Village Inn and McDonald's restaurants.

The Regency Inn is a deluxe facility with pool and sauna for visitors in the Hibbing area.

The 165-mile Taconite State Trail winds through scenic forests of aspen, birch and pine.

The only day of the year when the Taconite Trail is busy with skiers is during the Wilderness Trek, starting at the Ely golf course — an event that attracts skiers from all over Minnesota.

CHAPTER 11

STATE TRAILS

An extensive network of multiple-use trails across the Arrowhead region was authorized by the Minnesota Legislature in 1973. When completed, the entire system will traverse six counties, tie together five major population centers and either enter or provide access to nine state parks, thirteen state forest recreational areas, two national forest areas and one national park. The trails provide routes for both skiers and snowmobilers through some of the most picturesque and historically significant areas of the state. Because they are not specifically designated for cross-country skiers, however, they are not included among the trails that are described in detail in this guide. But, to not even mention them would be omitting noteworthy alternatives for skiers who prefer to avoid the nicely machine-groomed and track-set trails of the Arrowhead.

The state trails follow generally good, wide paths over gentle grades that do not necessitate sharp turns. The presence of both skiers and snowmobilers, however, may be a hazard to both. Snowmobiles are just as entitled to use the trails as are skiers. Be alert to their presence, and move off to the side of the trail when you see or hear one coming, because they may not see you.

Taconite Trail

The Taconite Trail stretches for 165 miles between Ely and Grand Rapids. The trail winds through scenic forests of birch, aspen and pine, past isolated lakes and streams, and near numerous points of historic interest, including old logging camps, deserted trappers shacks, and the first iron ore mine in Minnesota. Rustic wayside rests and picnic facilities enhance scenic vistas along the route. Among the ski trails included in this guide, those at McCarthy Beach State Park, Sturgeon River, the City of Tower and Bear Head Lake State Park are intersected by the Taconite State Trail.

North Shore Trail

The North Shore Trail follows the scenic north shore of Lake Superior for 153 miles between Duluth and Grand Marais. The trail winds through the beautiful highlands of the rugged Sawtooth Mountains, where lovely forests of birch, aspen, maple, spruce and pine enhance the "mountainous" terrain. Shelter huts are scattered along the trail, not more than ten miles apart, and there are numerous parking areas and access roads that break up the trail into appropriate day-long segments. The trail parallels (further inland) the entire North Shore Mountains Ski Trail and intersects access trails leading to Gooseberry Falls, Temperance River, Tettegouche, Crosby-Manitou and Cascade River state parks. Dozens of tourist accommodations, including resorts, motels, restaurants and service stations, are situated close to the trail.

FOR MORE INFORMATION: About state trails in the Arrowhead Region, contact the Minnesota Department of Natural Resources, Trails and Waterways Unit, Information Center, Box 40, 500 Lafayette Road, St. Paul, MN 55146. Or call TOLL FREE from within Minnesota 1-800-652-9747 (or locally 296-6699).

The Flathorn-Gegoka Ski Touring
Area harbors a fascinating variety
of forest habitats.

APPENDIX I

ARROWHEAD SKI TRAILS

NAME OF TRAIL:	GEOGRAPHIC REGION	LENGTH (miles)	DIFFI-CULTY	GRMD?	PAGE
1. Angleworm Lake — Spring Creek Loop	Echo Trail	16	A	No	167
2. Ashawa Ski Trail	Voyageur	39*	B,I,A	Yes	186
3. Ash River Trail	Voyageur	12.4	B,I,A	No	185
4. Astrid Lake Trails	Echo Trail	7	B,I	No	178
5. Bally Creek Trails	North Shore	5	B,I	Yes	81
6. Banadad Artery Trail	Gunflint Trail	16.2	I	Yes	108
7. Bass Lake Trail	Echo Trail	5.6	A	No	152
8. Bearhead Lake State Park	The Range	17	B,I,A	Yes	195
9. Big Aspen Trails	The Range	20.9	B,I.A.	Yes	204
10. Big Moose Trail	Echo Trail	4	I	No	173
11. Birch Lake Plantation	Ely	4.1	B,I	Yes	148
12. Bird Lake Trails	The Range	18	I,B,A	Yes	198
13. Black Bay Trail	Voyageur	8.6	B,I	No	184
14. Carey Lake Trail	The Range	3.5	B	Yes	213
15. Cascade River/ Deeryard Lake Trails	North Shore	32	I,B,A	Yes	79
16. Cascade River State Park	North Shore	13	I,B,A	Yes	59
17. Central Gunflint Trails	Gunflint Trail	25.5	I,B,A	Yes	103
18. City of Tower Ski Trail	The Range	6	I,B,A	Yes	195
19. Crane Lake Neighborhood Trail	Voyageur	5	B	Yes	187
20. Crane Lake Tower Trail	Voyageur	4	I	Yes	189
21. Fernberg Tower Trails	Ely	12.4	I	No	142
22. Flash Lake Trails	Ely	8	B,I	Yes	143
23. Flathorn-Gegoka Touring Area	Heart of Arrowhead	15	B,I	Yes	125
24. George H. Crosby Manitou State Park	North Shore	6	I,A	No	53
25. George Washington Memorial Pine Plantation	Gunflint Trail	1.5	B	No	101
26. Giants Ridge Ski Area	The Range	25	B,I,A	Yes	200
27. Good Harbor Bay Loop	North Shore	2.2	I,A	Yes	80
28. Gooseberry Falls State Park	North Shore	14.5	I,B,A	Yes	45
29. Grand Portage Area Trails	North Shore	99	I,B,A	Yes	89
30. Gunflint Lake Area Trails	Gunflint Trail	46	I,B,A	Yes	112
31. Hanson Lake Trail	Echo Trail	5	I	No	153
32. Hegman Lakes Trail	Echo Trail	4	I	No	163
33. Herriman Lake Trails	Voyageur	14.5	I	No	182
34. Hidden Valley Recreation Area	Ely	11.2	I,A	Yes	134
35. Jasper Hills Trails	Ely	14.5	I,B,A	Yes	138
36. Lookout Mountain Trail	The Range	14.7	I,A	Yes	206
37. Lutsen Mountains Ski Area	North Shore	22	I,A,B	Yes	76
38. Lutsen Ski Touring Center	North Shore	6	B,I	Yes	74
39. McCarthy Beach State Park	The Range	8.4	B,I,A	Yes	209
40. Moose Fence Trail	North Shore	4.8	I,B	Part	72
41. North Arm Trails	Echo Trail	34	I,B,A	No	157
42. North Junction Trails	Echo Trail	9.3	I,B	No	155
43. North Shore Mountains Ski Trail	North Shore	126	I,B,A	Yes	61
44. Northwoods Ski Trail	Heart of Arrowhead	9.3	B,I	Yes	123
45. Norway Trail	Echo Trail	16	I	No	173

APPENDIX I

ARROWHEAD SKI TRAILS (Continued)

NAME OF TRAIL:	GEOGRAPHIC REGION	LENGTH (miles)	DIFFI-CULTY	GRMD?	PAGE
46. Oberg Mountain Trail	North Shore	7.5	I,A	Yes	70
47. Pincushion Mountain Trails	Gunflint Trail	11.1	I,A,B	Yes	100
48. Sioux-Hustler Trails	Echo Trail	28	A	No	175
49. Solbakken Trails	North Shore	8	I	Yes	77
50. South Farm Lake Trails	Ely	6.8	B,I	Yes	135
51. Split Rock Lighthouse State Park	North Shore	6	B,I	Yes	47
52. Stuart Lake Trail	Echo Trail	16	I	No	171
53. Stuart River - Baldpate Lake Trails	Echo Trail	10	I,B	No	169
54. Sturgeon River Trail	The Range	20	B,I,A	No	207
55. Sugarbush Trail	North Shore	25.6	B,I,A	Yes	67
56. Temperance River State Park	North Shore	7.5	I,A,B	Yes	55
57. Tettegouche State Park	North Shore	12	I,A	Part	51
58. Thomas Lake Trail	Ely	11.2	A	No	146
59. Two Harbors City Trail	North Shore	6.5	B,I	Yes	43
60. Vic Power Park Trail	The Range	2	B	Yes	211
61. Woodland Caribou Trail	Heart of Arrowhead	20	I	No	127

(* Trails not completed in 1986, when this guide was published)

EXPLANATION OF APPENDIX:

#'s 1-61: Location of ski area on map insert inside back cover of book.

Geographic Region: The chapter describing the trail.

Length: Total skiing distance; on one-way trails, this is double the actual length of the trail.

Difficulty: B = Beginner, I = Intermediate, A = Advanced

Grmd?: Whether or not the trail is machine groomed and track-set.

Page: The page number on which the detailed description of the trail begins.

APPENDIX II

ARROWHEAD LODGING ACCOMMODATIONS

NAME OF RESORT:	GEOGRAPHIC REGION	LODGING OPTIONS	F	R	S	P	W	G	Page
A. Aurora Pines Motel	The Range	M,H							213
B. Bear Island Resort	Ely	H	X	X	X				149
C. Bearskin Lodge	Gunflint Trail	H,A	X	X	X		X		107
D. Beartrack Outfitting Company	North Shore	H	X		X				87
E. Bluefin Bay	North Shore	H	X	X			X		82
F. Borderland Lodge	Gunflint Trail	H, A	X		X				120
G. Boundary Country Trekking	Gunflint Trail	A,H	X		X				110
H. Bowser's Resort	Voyageur	M							191
I. Cascade Lodge	North Shore	M,H,A		X				X	86
J. Chateau Leveaux	North Shore	H,M	X		X	X	X	X	82
K. Cliff Dweller Resort	North Shore	M		X					83
L. Cobblestone Cabins	North Shore	H			X				83
M. Crane Lake Base Camp	Voyageur	H			X				191
N. Driftwood Lodge	Voyageur	H						X	192
O. East Bay Hotel	Gunflint Trail	M		X					102
P. Elbow Lake Lodge	Voyageur	H						X	190
Q. Escape (The)	Ely	H		X	X				150
R. Fenstad's Resort	North Shore	H	X		X				82
S. Golden Eagle Lodge	Gunflint Trail	H	X		X				107
T. Grand Portage Lodge	North Shore	M		X	X	X			97
U. Gull Harbor Condominums	North Shore	H	X		X		X	X	83
V. Gunflint Lodge	Gunflint Trail	H,A	X		X				119
W. Heston's Cabins	Gunflint Trail	H	X		X				120
X. Kec's Kove	Voyageur	H,A	X	X				X	193
Y. Lutsen Mountain Village	North Shore	H	X	X		X	X		83
Z. Lutsen Resort	North Shore	H,A,M	X	X	X	X	X	X	85
AA. Melgeorge's Resort	Voyageur	M		X					191
BB. National Forest Lodge	Heart of Arrowhead	H,A	X	X	X				131
CC. Northernaire Lodge	Ely	H,A	X	X	X			X	150
DD. Northwind Lodge	Ely	H			X				141
EE. Olson's Borderland Lodge	Voyageur	H		X	X				192
FF. Pine Aire Resort	Voyageur	H						X	192
GG. Regency Inn	The Range	M		X	X	X		X	215
HH. Rocky Point Resort	Voyageur	H,M,A		X					193
II. 'Sawtooth Mountain Lodge	Heart of Arrowhead	H			X				130
JJ. Scotwood Motel	The Range	M		X*					215
KK. Ski-View Motel	The Range	M			X				214
LL. Solbakken Resort	North Shore	H,M			X		X		86
MM. St. Paul YMCA Camps	Ely	H,A	X		X				161
NN. Sunset Resort	Voyageur	H,A		X				X	193
OO. Superior Forest Lodge	Ely	H			X			X	137
PP. Thomsonite Beach	North Shore	H	X						87
QQ. Thrifty Scot Motel	The Range	M		X*					215
RR. Thunderbird Lodge	Voyageur	H,M		X					193
SS. Voyageur North Motel	The Range	M							214

APPENDIX II

ARROWHEAD LODGING ACCOMMODATIONS (Continued)

EXPLANATION OF APPENDIX:

Letters A-SS: Location of resort on map insert inside back cover of book.

Geographic Region: The chapter describing the resort.

Lodging Options: M = Motel/Hotel Units, H = Housekeeping Units,
A = American Plan (or Modified Plan) availabe for meals.

Amenities: F = Fireplace or Wood Stove available
R = Restaurant open to the public
S = Sauna
P = Pool for swimming
W = Whirlpool, Jacuzzi bath
G = Games available

Page: The page number on which the detailed description of the resort begins.

(* Restaurant next door to lodging facility, not on premises.)

The summit of the Mt. Sophie Trail affords skiers an outstanding view of some of the most rugged landscape in the upper midwest.

The Crane Lake Neighborhood Trail passes through a dense forest of aspen.

The remote Woodland Caribou Trail is more likely to be tracked by timber wolves than by skiers.

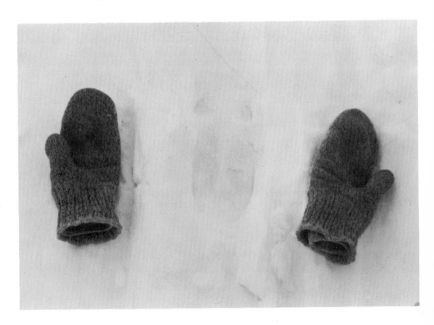

Moose tracks are frequently seen along the Banadad Artery Trail.